PETER HALL DIRECTS
Antony and Cleopatra

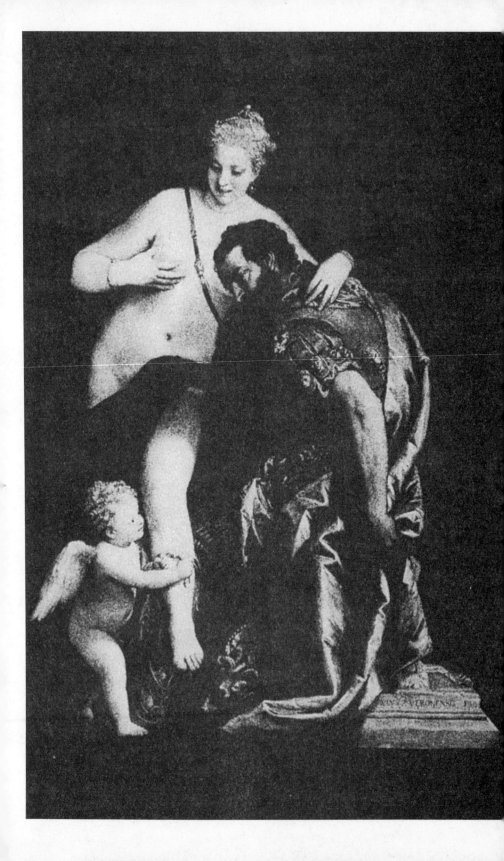

TIRZAH LOWEN

PETER HALL DIRECTS
Antony and Cleopatra

---

with photographs by John Haynes

82J
33
01L

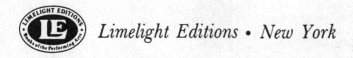

Limelight Editions • New York

First Limelight Edition February 1991

First published in Great Britain in 1990 by Methuen Drama
Michelin House 81 Fulham Road, London SW3 6RB

Library of Congress Cataloging-in-Publication Data

Lowen, Tirzah.
    Peter Hall directs Antony and Cleopatra / Tirzah Lowen.—1st
Limelight ed.
        p.   cm.
    Includes index.
    ISBN 0-87910-141-5   ISBN 0-87910-147-4
    1. Shakespeare, William, 1564–1616. Antony and Cleopatra.
2. Cleopatra, Queen of Egypt, d. 30 B.C., in fiction, drama, poetry,
etc.   3. Antonius, Marcus, 83?–30 B.C., in fiction, drama, poetry,
etc.   4. Shakespeare, William, 1564–1616—Dramatic production.
5. Hall, Peter, Sir, 1930–   I. Title.
PR2802.L69 1990   90-36644   CIP
822.3'3—dc20

In Memory of My Father
EPHRAIM LOEWENSTEIN

Acknowledgements: Above all, to Peter Hall and his actors, who tolerated my presence at what is normally a very private experience

To the stage management, Ernie Hall, Paul Greaves, Angie Bissett and Emma Lloyd, who, no matter how busy, were always accessible and a rich source of information

To the creative team, Alison Chitty, Dominic Muldowney, Stephen Wentworth and Paul Arditti, and to Malcolm Ranson and Julia Wilson-Dixon, all of whom allowed themselves to be 'interrogated'

To John Goodwin, for his advice and his kindness, and to his assistant Liz Curry, for more of the same

To Lynn Haill and her colleagues in the print office, to Nicki Frei, Jan Younghusband, Gillian Diamond, Josette Nicholls, Ghita Cohen, and all those in the costume, construction and technical departments who gave me their valuable time

To Nic, Josette, Maureen and Linda at the Stage Door, for their unfailing assistance and efficiency

To Rick Witcombe, writer and friend, generous with enlivening suggestions, a much-needed sounding board

To the best of agents, Jennifer Watts

And to Ken, who encouraged and supported me through the months of writing

Finally, I return to Peter Hall, to thank him for an enduring gift – he truly opened the door to Shakespeare's language

CONTENTS

LIST OF ILLUSTRATIONS

The photographs listed below were all taken by John Haynes and the drawings were taken from designer Alison Chitty's sketchbook. They are reproduced here with their kind permission.

Illustrations between pp. 32 and 33

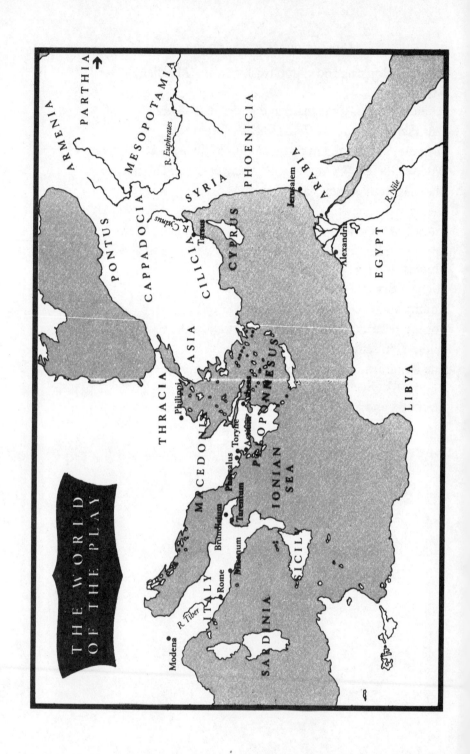

THE WORLD OF THE PLAY

PARTHIA
ARMENIA
MESOPOTAMIA
R. Euphrates
CAPPADOCIA
PONTUS
SYRIA
R. Cydnus
Tarsus
CILICIA
PHOENICIA
Jerusalem
ARABIA
CYPRUS
ASIA
Alexandria
EGYPT
THRACIA
Philippi
LIBYA
MACEDONIA
Toryne
PELOPONNESUS
Pharsalus
Actium
Naxos
Brundisium
IONIAN
Tarentum
SEA
Misenum
SICILY
Rome
R. Tiber
ITALY
SARDINIA
Modena

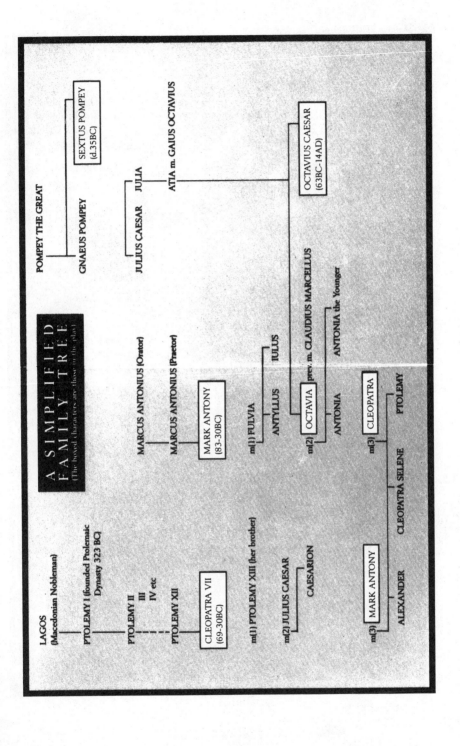

A SIMPLIFIED FAMILY TREE
(The boxed characters are those in the play)

POMPEY THE GREAT

GNAEUS POMPEY

SEXTUS POMPEY (d.35BC)

JULIUS CAESAR   JULIA

ATIA m GAIUS OCTAVIUS

OCTAVIUS CAESAR (63BC-14AD)

MARCUS ANTONIUS (Orator)

MARCUS ANTONIUS (Praetor)

MARK ANTONY (83-30BC)

m1) FULVIA

ANTYLLUS

IULUS

OCTAVIA prev. m. CLAUDIUS MARCELLUS

ANTONIA the Younger

m(2) OCTAVIA

ANTONIA

m(3) CLEOPATRA

PTOLEMY

CLEOPATRA SELENE

LAGOS (Macedonian Nobleman)

PTOLEMY I (founded Ptolemaic Dynasty 323 BC)

PTOLEMY II
III
IV etc

PTOLEMY XII

CLEOPATRA VII (69-30BC)

m(1) PTOLEMY XIII (her brother)

m(2) JULIUS CAESAR

CAESARION

m(3) MARK ANTONY

ALEXANDER

Peter Hall's production of *Antony and Cleopatra* opened on 9 April 1987 in the Olivier Theatre. The company was as follows:

Rulers of the Roman world:

Mark Antony	**Anthony Hopkins**
Octavius Caesar	**Tim Pigott-Smith**
Lepidus	**John Bluthal**

Antony's friends and followers:

Domitius Enobarbus	**Michael Bryant**
Philo	**Mike Hayward**
Eros	**Jeremy Flynn**
Ventidius	**Brian Spink**
Scarus	**Andrew C. Wadsworth**
Canidius	**Daniel Thorndike**
Silius	**Desmond Adams**
Decretas	**Michael Carter**

Caesar's friends and followers:

Octavia, *Caesar's sister*	**Sally Dexter**
Agrippa	**Basil Henson**
Demetrius	**Brian Spink**
Maecenas	**Graham Sinclair**
Thidias	**Desmond Adams**
Dolabella	**Andrew C. Wadsworth**
Proculeius	**Brian Spink**
Gallus	**Desmond Adams**
Lady attending on Octavia	**Frances Quinn**
Sextus Pompey	**David Schofield**

Pompey's allies:

Menecrates	**Peter Gordon**
Menas	**Michael Carter**
Varrius	**Michael Bottle**
Boy	**Peter Corey** or **Paul Vinhas**
Cleopatra	**Judi Dench**

Cleopatra's court:

Charmian	**Miranda Foster**
Iras	**Helen Fitzgerald**
Alexas	**Robert Arnold**
Clown	**John Bluthal**
Mardian	**Iain Ormsby-Knox**
Diomedes	**Robert Arnold**

Seleucus	**Daniel Thorndike**
Schoolmaster	**Peter Gordon**
Soothsayer	**Daniel Thorndike**
Egyptian	**Michael Bottle**

Messengers and Soldiers:
Ian Bolt, Patrick Brennan, Hus Levent, Simon Needs, Simon Scott

Musicians:
Michael Brain (*bombard, flute, pipes*),
Michael Gregory (*drums*),
Howard Hawkes (*trumpet*),
Colin Rae (*trumpet*),
Roderick Skeaping, Nicholas Hayley (*violin, rebec*),
David Tosh (*drums*),
George Weigand (*lute, oud, archcittern*)

Director	**Peter Hall**
Designer	**Alison Chitty**
Lighting	**Stephen Wentworth**
Music	**Dominic Muldowney**
Sound Design	**Paul Arditti**
Action Supervisor	**Malcolm Ranson**
Voice Coach	**Julia Wilson-Dixon**
Staff Director	**Alan Cohen**
Production Manager	**Michael Cass-Jones**

Stage Manager	**Ernest Hall**
Deputy Stage Manager	**Angela Bissett**
Asst. Stage Managers	**Paul Greaves**
	Emma B. Lloyd
Design Assistant	**David Neat**
Asst. Lighting Design	**Paul McLeish**
Asst. Prod. Manager	**George Ellerington**
Costume Supervisors	**Stephanie Baird**
	Anna Watkins
Production photographed by	**John Haynes**

PREFACE

PHILO: Nay, but this dotage of our general's
O'erflows the measure.
. . . His captain's heart
Which in the scuffle of great fights hath burst
The buckles on his breast, reneges all temper
And is become the bellows and the fan
To cool a gypsy's lust.

Look where they come
Take but good note and you shall see in him
The triple pillar of the world transformed
Into a strumpet's fool.

Act One, Scene 1

I am as much interested in the making of a piece of theatre as by what finally appears onstage. Can one explain the creative process? It is presumptuous even to try, but by describing the steps taken, one may convey some of its magic.

In 1984, I read Peter Hall's *Diaries** and was fascinated, not only by his account, as helmsman of the National Theatre, of steering it through the rapids which beset its early years on the South Bank, but by what was revealed of a man also struggling to maintain his individual creativity, prey to all the crises of confidence and in-securities of the artist.

One passage, in particular, connected: '. . . why I do this job. Not for performance – not for plays – not for money – but for the satisfaction of having a really good rehearsal where the excitement of discovery spreads from actor to actor'.

I wrote to ask whether I could sit in on a play he was directing. We

* Editor John Goodwin (Hamish Hamilton, London, 1983)

kept in touch and when *Antony and Cleopatra* was scheduled for early 1987, with Anthony Hopkins and Judi Dench in the name parts, it seemed ideal from every point of view. It is a play I love – just as well: I would be watching it take shape through thirteen long weeks . . .

WEEK I – DAY I – Monday 12 January 1987

A mean day of icy roads, sub-zero temperatures. Almost fifty people assemble round a vast conference table on the fourth floor of the National Theatre – actors, stage management, designers, David Aukin, the NT's Executive Director, Ann Robinson from Casting, the production's publicist, Nicki Frei, and its director, Peter Hall, dark-suited, smiling and deeply preoccupied. Beneath the greetings, anecdotes and laughter is the tension of having soon to show one's hand.

At 10.30 the director makes a start, setting *Antony and Cleopatra* against its world-embracing canvas. Since the colour and tone is Renaissance, designer Alison Chitty wants to create a sixteenth-century view of the classical world – 'with not a bare knee or snake headdress in sight'.

Referring to the lush language of the play: the actors should learn to handle the verse correctly. 'If you approach it psychologically, it will get up and hit you!' warns Hall.

Everyone listens closely: it is Hall who created the Royal Shakespeare Company, who, with his colleagues, revolutionized the approach to Shakespeare and his contemporaries. He hands over to his actors for a first reading.

Anthony Hopkins, grey-bearded for *King Lear*, and Judi Dench, with her cap of blonde hair, are strikingly matched in physical type. Both wear glasses. When they start to speak, their voices are similarly warm and husky, his Welsh-accented, hers with a distinctive and appealing break to it.

At lunchtime Hall has an NT meeting. Based on his decision of several months before (to leave the National when his contract expires in September 1988), the media the next day reveal that the Board and he have chosen Richard Eyre to succeed him as director of the NT.

WEEK 1 – Wednesday 14 January

They begin to 'block' the moves of the play. Some directors arrive with everything planned. Peter Hall tells of doing *Cymbeline* when he was twenty-six, with a cast which included Peggy Ashcroft. It was his first job at Stratford and he had meticulously worked out each move beforehand, so that by the fifth day most of the play had been covered: 'Then, nose to my notes, I told Dame Peggy to walk right across the stage. This she dutifully wrote down and did. A few seconds later, she said gently, "Peter, that isn't right." As director, a new one at that, I had a quick decision to make: either to assert myself – or rethink . . . . We scrapped every move and went back to the beginning.' Never since then has he blocked a play without the collaboration of his actors.

WEEK 2 – Tuesday 20 January

They move into Rehearsal Room 1, which approximates to the Olivier stage in size. Black-slatted walls contain the vastness. The only natural light comes through dormer windows high in the roof.

Anthony Hopkins is relentless about needing to understand every word, every line of thought. He beats out the accents of the iambic pentameter, runs back over lines trying different emphases. (Sometimes, early mornings, he sits at a piano in the corner, playing Scriabin and improvising.)

Michael Bryant addresses him affectionately as 'Dai Welly'. Bryant, playing Enobarbus, has been at the National since 1977. In his customary grey track-suit, glasses on a cord round his neck, snuff-box in pocket, he seems part of the fabric of the building itself. I have a vision of him living in his dressing-room. . . . In his work he digs for the reality, the humanity of a character, cutting incisively through words to feeling and sense.

It is tricky to hold in balance both the 'mathematics' of the verse, and the emotion and thought behind it. Hall compares it to jazz: 'You can do anything you like with it, once you have found the beat.' The actors find the challenge exhilarating, Tim Pigott-Smith (Caesar) amongst them. This actor's profile and bearing have become identified with such 'menace' roles as Merrick in *Jewel in the Crown* but he attacks new ideas with boyish enthusiasm, is a great giggler and mimic.

WEEK 2 – Wednesday 21 January

News that *Antony and Cleopatra* will go to Epidaurus in July, be performed in Egypt, near the pyramids, in October delights everyone.

Having challenged Caesar to fight in single combat and been turned down, Antony is like a bull, looking for something to gore. Peter Hall enacts this, hunching his shoulders, glowering, pawing the ground. Catches it exactly. Later he pantomimes five servants bowing and scraping. After lunch, he's in high spirits, bustling the actors along, telling anecdotes, sending up to his office for a cigar ('I ought to give them up. No, not health – it's the cost'). He is so focused on these rehearsals that it is a shock to be reminded that he is also carrying the overall reponsibility for the NT (an urgent letter is sent in for signature, he has to be chivvied away to a television discussion on the need for arts subsidy, returns from a lunchtime meeting with a group of American critics). Taking home a bag of paperwork each night, he returns in the mornings, usually before anyone else in his office, all of it dealt with. He also sees first rehearsals, run-throughs, previews and first nights of every other production in the repertoire, giving notes to actors and directors. I spoke to Jan Younghusband, once his assistant, by 1987 handling the intricacies of scheduling the repertoire: in seven years she has never heard him raise his voice – he faces problems realistically, invites opinions, is delighted with initiative. His administrative coterie, aware of the huge demands made on him, are continually astounded by his ability to give absolute attention to whatever he is dealing with. That he is now revelling in the rehearsal process of *Antony and Cleopatra* is because 'He's doing what he's here for, with a play he loves'.

WEEK 2 – Thursday 22 January

Under the repertoire system which operates at the National, two or three plays alternate each week in each of its three auditoria. As I arrive at the National at 9.30 a.m., there is a queue at the Box Office for the forty sold-on-the-day seats for *King Lear*. In the foyer of the Cottesloe, sixty schoolchildren performing in *The Pied Piper* are changing for the morning performance. At the Stage Door phones are buzzing, mail is being sorted and actors are signing in. There is also a cross-section of reviews from the previous night's opening of *Three Men on a Horse*. Irving Wardle in *The Times* calls it 'A great night out!' The *Financial Times* is lukewarm; did they see the same production? Up in the canteen, stage staff and actors are breakfasting, amongst them Michael Gambon, gesturing and talking to himself as he goes over his lines for *A View from the Bridge*, currently in rehearsal.

WEEK 3 – Wednesday 28 January

Judi Dench first worked with Hall in *A Midsummer Night's Dream* at Stratford, in 1962. She is very feminine, small neat hands covered with rings, and rehearsing, warm, open, sometimes deeply pensive. With that plangent, unique voice it would be easy to move listeners with an inflection, but no effect is cheaply achieved, there is effort and intelligence behind everything she does. I try hard to see the seam between technical skill and emotion dredged up from the gut – and can't. She is also briskly funny: after a photo session for a newspaper interview, for example, 'What they wanted was me on a chaise with an asp. What they got was a cross face in a leather coat.' Rebutting the concern Dench had expressed about the age of Cleopatra (38 to her own 52), what comes across is radiance, vulnerability, and movement that is quick, light and youthful.

WEEK 3 – Friday 30 January

Peter Hall works on a scene in which the Roman Triumvirate, Antony, Caesar and Lepidus (played by John Bluthal, probably best known for his television comedy roles) meet Pompey to negotiate peace. Pompey is played by David Schofield, a very physical actor, superb as the original 'Elephant Man', now playing a song-and-dance man in *The American Clock* at the NT. Hall talks of the absolute sincerity and courtesy of political liars: 'The only difference is that then they used swords.'

Later, the director proposes that they do the banquet scene on Pompey's galley as if they are all drunk. Eight grown men proceed to go into such paroxysms of raucous inebriation, leaning on one another, falling about, slurring and belching, that soon everyone, watching and performing, is clutching themselves with laughter. Through it, discoveries will have been made, elements will be preserved.

WEEK 4

The actors have a week off to learn lines, during which work on the set and costume designs, props, programme notes and poster continues.

WEEK 5 – Monday 9 February

Peter Hall is very slow to force the staging. He lets actors feel their way through the sense, their feelings and (newly learned) words before finally making a suggestion.

Other actors watch, mesmerized, as Hall leads Tony Hopkins gently through Antony's decision to kill himself and be reunited with Cleopatra (whom he believes to be dead). From the actor there is trust and dependency, from the director guidance and reassurance. The actor needs the director as a sounding board. Conversely, having set the ball rolling, Hall asks to be surprised by his actors' revelations.

WEEK 6 – Monday 16 February

Adding to the opening scene of the play: the Egyptian court. There is nothing half-hearted about Hopkins as, brandishing a wine flagon and goblet, he goes all out, exploring each new possibility to its limits, experimenting and taking risks. 'The outrageous gambolling of two middle-aged lovers should be shocking,' approves Hall.

WEEK 7 – Wednesday 25 February

Responding to Antony's humiliating defeat at the battle of Actium, Peter Hall comments: 'God knows it's happened to me. The morning after a big failure, how do you behave? You meet your friends and whatever they do, it hurts. If they say nothing, you're embarrassed, if they offer sympathy, you don't want it. That's why I always pull the sheets over my head!'

WEEK 7 – Thursday 26 February

There is a run-through of the first half of the play. The scenes begin to lock into one another, to make connections. The stage is kept constantly 'hot', filled with action as actors walk, stride, run on in a new scene as those in the previous one make their exits.

Simon Scott, a latecomer to the *Antony and Cleopatra* company, had been given several lines as a Messenger the day before: as he delivers them from memory, his voice is strong and clear – his legs are visibly shaking. . . .

When Cleopatra learns of Antony's marriage to Octavia, new moves, inventiveness, come naturally out of Dench's emotion. She rises to tremendous anger and then dissolves into racking, almost childlike sobs. Tears run down her cheeks. The pain she communicates is transfixing.

At the end of the day, Peter Brook drops in to see Peter Hall. They talk warmly, in an undertone.

WEEK 7 – Friday 27 February

The morning of the snake auditions. A slow-worm and a black racer have been brought in, to be tried out as Cleopatra's asps. Everyone crowds round as Dench and Miranda Foster (Charmian) learn how to handle them. The racer is decided upon. The slow-worm goes very quiet. Murmurs gentle Ernie Hall, chief stage manager: 'Well, wouldn't you, if you'd just lost a job?' I wonder at this sudden call for naturalism in an emblematic production.

WEEK 8 – Friday 6 March

Late afternoon. It is quiet in the vast rehearsal room. Very few people are about – four actors, the director, two stage managers. Hall works with David Schofield, feeding in ideas sparked off by another run-through: 'Sorry, it's my fault for not realizing before: Pompey's language is full of sexual distaste. He wants to take over the world and close all the brothels. So keep it driven, crisp – and dangerous. What we want to avoid is the tone of braggadocio. . . .'

When at last they think they've cracked the scene, 'It's awful,' he says. 'If you dig far enough, the truth is always there. While I was at the RSC, the critics talked of social relevance, physical energy. In fact, it was largely to do with speaking the text correctly.'

It is six o'clock, at the end of a long week. Nobody wants to leave. They stand round the director, asking questions, exchanging ideas. Thoughtful, responsive, he seems to have no other calls on his time. This is Hall, the ruthless tyrant of the South Bank? For his actors he is a generous father-figure, providing a net of security within which they have the freedom to explore.

WEEK 9 – Wednesday 11 March

Those unsung heroes, the stage management. A day spent in the Olivier Theatre. Banner and drum processions through the aisles. Eyes glued to his marked-up script, Paul Greaves prompts, reads in for an absent actor, provides background drumming, indicates music, battle sounds at sea, distant cheers. Emma Lloyd deals with all the props, distributes the right shields, halberds and swords to the multiple points of entrance. She and Angie Bissett (who is also arranging the innumerable costume fittings) operate the mobile sections of the set. Ernie Hall, 'lynch-pin' of the production, supervises. As is sometimes suggested, stage management as well as actors should take a curtain call.

WEEK 10 – Thursday 19 March

Basil Henson has been an actor since 1946, with the National since 1978. Lean, trim, military in manner and bearing, he is well cast as

Agrippa, Caesar's general. He and Michael Bryant have a Tweedledum/Tweedledee act which goes on today:

Bryant: (after Henson's delayed entrance) Oh, I didn't know you were being *sensitive* out there.

Henson: I wasn't. I was giving you a *meaningful* pause.

Bryant: We could have been through this scene if you pulled yourself together.

Henson: But there are *subtle* alternatives . . . I'll need to put in a 'then' before I speak. . . .

Bryant: But you can't do that in Shakespeare, Bas, that's *RSC* style. We can't have that. . . .

WEEK 10 – Friday 20 March

Tony Hopkins, attacking a scene: 'How can I get it without making all that noise?', causes empathetic laughter.

WEEK 11 – Monday 23 March

Time is running out. As the first public preview approaches, tension mounts. Sitting in the canteen which looks out onto the Thames, Peter Hall recalls his early problem-filled years at the National: 'Sometimes, working in my office here at 3.00 in the morning, I'd pray it would all burn down . . . .'

WEEK 11 – Friday 27 March

Eleven weeks into rehearsal. The next will be largely technical, with the adjustment to sets, costumes, lights and sound.

The week culminates in the first complete run-through in the Olivier itself. The action has opened out to fill stage and auditorium. There are great patches of vitality and stature. Dominic Muldowney's evocative music gives a taste of what all the effects will add.

And just a week from today, this production will unfurl before its first paying audience.

INTRODUCTION
The Framework and Casting

The National Theatre on the South Bank, overlooking the River Thames, was officially opened by the Queen on 25 October 1976, under the directorship of Peter Hall (who was knighted the following year).

The concept of a British National Theatre was first proposed by a London publisher, Effingham Wilson, in 1848. Over the next century, it was variously revived and fought for by Matthew Arnold, Harley Granville Barker, George Bernard Shaw and Winston Churchill and others.

In 1949, the National Theatre Bill allowed for government to pay up to £1 million for the project. In 1969, after several changes of site, building work started on the South Bank near the Festival Hall, by which time costs were estimated to be £7,500,000. By the time of final completion in early 1977, these costs amounted to £25.7 million. The architect was Sir Denys Lasdun, working in conjunction with Theatre Projects, consultants for the stage engineering, lighting and sound.

In the meantime, since 22 October 1963 (when Peter O'Toole opened in *Hamlet*) an officially named National Theatre had been operating very successfully at a temporary home at the Old Vic. For ten years its artistic director was Sir Laurence Olivier, from whom Peter Hall took over in November 1973.

After leaving Cambridge, Hall had started off reading scripts and assisting, for £7 a week, at the Arts Theatre in London. Director there himself from 1955, he went on to freelance in the West End and with regional theatres, amongst them the Shakespeare Memorial Theatre at Stratford. Appointed its director in 1959, at the age of twenty-eight, he founded the Royal Shakespeare Company, soon to be considered the finest and most exciting ensemble in Britain. He gathered a permanent nucleus of actors and added to the Stratford theatre a London base, the Aldwych, for staging mainly modern plays and non-Shakespeare classics. With colleagues John Barton, Peter Brook and Michel Saint-Denis – later joined by Trevor Nunn, David Jones, Clifford Williams and Terry Hands – Hall developed a house style of selective naturalism (his words), textual truth, and enormous freshness and vigour. It was a happy marriage of the intellectual and emotional, which revitalized the approach to Shakespeare and his contemporaries, and influenced the production of modern-day playwrights like Albee, Pinter and Genet. Although the RSC was said to be a directors' theatre, a generation of actors like David Warner, Judi Dench, Vanessa Redgrave, Diana Rigg, Alan Howard, Ian Richardson and Ian Holm developed there in the sixties, to become the hallmark of British ensemble playing.

After ten years with the RSC, Peter Hall left to freelance as a theatre and film director, whilst also attached to the Royal Opera. On the point of becoming its co-director in 1971, he had second thoughts, and resigned. Soon afterwards, he was asked to succeed Olivier at the National. Almost overwhelming problems came with the job: funding was short and delays on the new building seemingly interminable, exacerbated by the severe economic recession of 1973/74.

In an effort to force the complex into existence as soon as possible, and before the entire building was anything like complete, each of the three theatres within the National was opened as it became available: the proscenium-arched Lyttelton, with 890 seats, on 8 March 1976 (with a week of plays transferred from the Old Vic), the fan-shaped, open-staged Olivier, seating 1,160, on 4 October (with Albert Finney in *Tamburlaine the Great*) and, finally, the flexi-space 400-seated Cottesloe, on 4 March 1977 (with Ken Campbell's eight-hour *Illuminatus*, visiting from Liverpool).

The period of adjustment from the Old Vic to the new South Bank complex was far from easy. Protracted building delays meant that the repertoire of plays built up in preparation for the move had to be kept on ice. This caused scheduling problems and a mood of uncertainty – actors could not be kept on indefinitely. There were technical problems with sophisticated stage equipment: to compensate for mechanical failings, extra stage crews had to be taken on. This was an added financial burden and lowered morale. Union strikes disrupted the repertoire, reduced much-needed box office income and sapped energy. The actual running costs of the building, impossible to estimate accurately prior to its opening, proved high. In the first year of occupancy, the NT required an extra £500,000 of government funding to cover its heavy costs – and this at a time when other subsidized theatres were suffering cutbacks and struggling for their very survival. There was acrimony in the profession, and the media generally were full of almost gleeful criticism, getting headline mileage out of every setback. At times, as fully documented in Peter Hall's published *Diaries* of the period (1972–1980), it seemed pointless to try and continue against apparently insurmountable odds.

Yet gradually the beast was tamed. By 1987, when *Antony and Cleopatra* went into rehearsal, the mammoth complex had become an indispensable part of the national and, indeed, international theatre spectrum, its foyers crowded, lively and informal, open all day, six days a week, offering exhibitions, bookshops, buffets and early-evening concerts, the three auditoria at its core filled with audiences of 80 per cent capacity (overall), for close to 1,200 performances a year.

Making the whole operation function was a full-time staff of 550 people (including artistic and administrative management, script, publicity and marketing departments, technical and constructional teams, front-of-house, catering and box-office staff and maintenance engineers) plus a company of almost 150 actors.

In 1987 a triumvirate shared the decision-making: Hall himself, David Aukin (Executive Director) and John Faulkner (Head of Artistic Planning). They were responsible to a Board which 'works extremely hard and works us extremely hard' (Faulkner). General administration of the organization was divided between Douglas Gosling (Head of Finance) and Aukin.

There were lengthy consultations about the National's repertoire of productions. This is normally scheduled two years ahead, in some flexible detail for the current year, in outline for the year to follow, and it was Jan Younghusband's responsibility to chart the programme, both longterm and day-to-day. She got feedback from different departments (such as marketing, if the play was a set work for schools) and had to consider a range of factors: because of the drain on energy and voice, actors carrying leading roles were consulted about how many shows they would do in a week. An actor cannot be rehearsing two plays at once – or performing in them on the self-same night. (A notable exception was Basil Henson: playing in both *Pravda* and *Dalliance*, it worked out that he could scoot between the two in an evening!)

Initially, a play is scheduled for six months ahead. Its success, of course, cannot be predicted: on one occasion a production was pulled out after only two weeks, but normally the scheduling of a play which is not doing well is adjusted to accommodate its widest potential audience (matinée-goers, perhaps, or weekenders). Similar adjustments are made for a hit, and the public receives the finalized programme of the repertoire in the NT's booking leaflets at six-weekly intervals. 'The schedule,' says Younghusband, 'is a flexible, adjustable, amendable tool; its purpose – to balance the artistic demands of the company with public demand.'

From the beginning, Peter Hall had wanted the National Theatre to present as much variety as possible, to be a reflection of the nation's theatre. The greater the diversity of material on offer, the greater the opportunity for different approaches, not just those representing the ideas of one man.

From October 1984, it was possible to implement an obvious extension to that thinking: rather than attempt to forge a single instrument from an amorphous company, to cope with every theatrical need, the NT was separated into five groups led by different directors. Each director would select twenty to twenty-five actors to do a minimum of three plays over the following year, one in each of the three theatres, tailoring material to actors and vice versa.

This has obvious attractions: for directors and actors it offers a variety of work, in different spaces, within an ensemble framework, and for an audience the emergent cohesion of each group becomes deeply satisfying. Hall also believes that it is the most economical way to run the building, using resources to their fullest. Just as he had done at the RSC in the sixties, he has put his mark firmly on the National.

The self-evident success of the group idea leads one to forget that the company ever functioned differently – just as one might easily forget that the South Bank complex has not always been there to enjoy.

*

When, on Monday 12 January 1987, rehearsals for *Antony and Cleopatra* started, the plays already running in the National's three auditoria were *King Lear*, *Animal Farm*, *The Pied Piper*, Arthur Miller's *The American Clock*, the new Stephen Poliakoff, *Coming in to Land*, Pinero's *The Magistrate*, the 1920s farce *Tons of Money* and *Bopha!* (a visiting production from South Africa's Market Theatre). The 1930s Broadway comedy *Three Men on a Horse* was poised to open in the Cottesloe, *School for Wives* in the Lyttelton. *A View from the Bridge* and *Six Characters in Search of an Author* were also in rehearsal, as were several early-evening Platform Performances and workshop productions from the NT Studio, run by Peter Gill.

Coming in to Land had had its Press Night only four days before. With scarce time to digest audience and critics' response, the same team – director Peter Hall, his designer Alison Chitty, his staff director Alan Cohen, the stage management and four of the actors – switched their focus to *Antony and Cleopatra*.

A generous thirteen-week rehearsal schedule lay ahead, but one which would have to take account of other demands: actors and stage management who would be unavailable whenever they had matinées, word-runs, understudy and cast-replacement rehearsals for plays already in the repertoire, and union requirements that actors be given a two-hour break between rehearsing and performing, and a twelve-hour break following an evening performance. That actors due to perform at night rehearse for no more than six hours (including lunchbreak) during the day, would add to the jigsaw of daily planning.

The week before rehearsals started, the 'Contact' department of the NT mailed out almost 40,000 leaflets to subscribers, with booking information for the March/April period, during which *Antony and Cleopatra* would preview and open:

> "All for love – or the world well lost." The destructive
> passion of two great lovers on the brink of middle age, is
> set against the political dissolution of the entire
> Mediterranean world.

Sobering synchronicity: the actors would just be feeling their way into the play, as the public began to buy tickets to see it.

*

This production had first been mooted two years before. Staff director Cohen claims that it was during a technical rehearsal for *Coriolanus*. Gazing idly at its sandpit-like set whilst lights were being adjusted, Hall and he considered how many other Shakespearean plays could be done on it . . . *Antony and Cleopatra*, for one – and that spark ignited.

The National had never done the play before. Neither had Hall, but since he considers it to be 'probably the greatest play in the language . . . the most comprehensive and universal of Shake-speare's tragedies', it was more a question of when rather than if he would ever direct it.

He had first seen *Antony and Cleopatra* in the forties, done by the Marlowe Society, and then by Edith Evans and Godfrey Tearle at the Piccadilly: 'I waited so long to do the play myself because I couldn't cast it. The casting is critical. You have to find two actors who can embody what is said about them – in terms of charisma – as well as two who can handle some of the most difficult language in Shake-speare.'

Judi Dench says that Hall first mentioned the possibility of her doing a Cleopatra for him when she was at the National four years before (since when the idea had 'very usefully incubated' in a corner of her mind).

Dench grew up in York, the daughter of a doctor. She chose to become a Quaker, a factor which has profoundly influenced her life and work. Soon after she left drama school in 1957, she played Ophelia to John Neville's Hamlet at the Old Vic, and a legendary Juliet directed by Zeffirelli, after which Peter Hall cast her as Titania at Stratford. During an illustrious career, she has done almost all the Shakespearean female leads, some of them more than once, many during her long association with the RSC – but never Cleopatra. Her range is exceptional: other parts include Anya – and Madame Ranyevskaya – in *The Cherry Orchard*, Major Barbara, St Joan, Sally Bowles in the musical *Cabaret*, Millament in *The Way of the World*, Juno in *Juno and the Paycock*, Lady Bracknell and Mother Courage. More recently have come film roles, one after the other, and bags of fan-mail following *A Fine Romance*, the 26-part TV comedy series she starred in with her husband, Michael Williams.

At the time she returned to the National to work on Hall's production, she was also doing *Mr and Mrs Nobody* with Williams, at the Garrick Theatre. Its guaranteed stop-date would release her for the last two rehearsal weeks and the run of *Antony and Cleopatra*. Until then she would continue to give nine performances a week (including matinées) in the West End, whilst rehearsing Cleopatra on the South Bank.

Anthony Hopkins, a baker's son from Port Talbot in Wales, established himself early as an actor of charismatic presence. Unlike Dench, he has had a love-hate relationship with British theatre, in 1975 abandoning it, seemingly for ever, to move to America. Before that, he had done memorable work on television (his Pierre in *War and Peace* gained the BAFTA Best TV Actor award) and had been cutting a swathe through leading roles at the National (then at the Old Vic), until a clash with director John Dexter made him walk out. Feeling his name with the National was blackened for good, he went off to New York where his first triumph was in *Equus* – directed by Dexter!

Ten years later, having become a star of Hollywood films (*A Bridge Too Far*, *The Elephant Man*, *Magic*, and *The Bounty*, for which he got a Best Film Actor award), he quietly returned to England and was doing a play by Schnitzler when David Hare invited him to rejoin the National (now on the South Bank) for *Pravda*.

As a result of the play's – and his – great success (as newspaper magnate Lambert Le Roux) his contract was twice extended as the production ran on and on. He followed that with *King Lear*, became the obvious choice for an Antony – and a reason for slotting the play into the NT repertoire for 1987. Peter Hall had never lost faith in him as 'a great actor in the British tradition'.

Once the two leads were in place, the other roles could be cast. Having had a long association with Hall, the NT's then Head of Casting, Gillian Diamond, was familiar with the kind of actor he liked. Whilst he was directing *Coming in to Land*, she and her colleague Anne Robinson communicated with him via innumerable notes and lists, and the cast of twenty-eight was culled almost entirely from actors already performing in other productions at the National.

The few additions from outside were Jerry Flynn, John Bluthal and Simon Scott (all of whom had worked at the National before), Frances Quinn and Iain Ormsby-Knox. Cheerful and burly, with the high, sweet singing voice needed for the part of the eunuch Mardian,

Ormsby-Knox was only contacted the week rehearsals began. He travelled down from Stoke-on-Trent, was interviewed, did a sight-reading, and came straight in to start work with the company, looking slightly dazed.

The numerous generals, ambassadors, and smaller attendant and messenger parts caused a problem for the casting department: they require strong presence and delivery but actors are disappointed not to get a bite at something bigger. Andrew Wadsworth, with a background of leads in West End musicals and at the National, wandered unhappily in and out of rehearsals until he (and his agent) arrived at a combination of small but weighty parts of which he could make something.

There was great casting skill in this 'doubling', to cover the forty speaking characters in *Antony and Cleopatra*. Sometimes there is a line through the roles – Wadsworth, for instance, plays two 'gallants', Scarus and Dolabella, Brian Spink plays a succession of dignified Romans, Michael Carter, the pirate Menas and piratical Decretas, and Desmond Adams is the sober Silius and the diplomat Thidias. Elsewhere, an actor has been cast in challengingly contrasted parts, as is John Bluthal (as the triumvir Lepidus and the rural Clown at the end of the play) and Peter Gordon, who is Menecrates the pirate and then the gentle Schoolmaster. As an ensemble, most of the cast will also swell the army ranks and play assorted messengers or servants.

As well, every role is understudied within the company: Sally Dexter, whose 'principal' part is Octavia, is also the understudy for Cleopatra. Were she to have to go on instead of Judi Dench, Frances Quinn would replace her as Octavia.

Several young actors had been taken on the year before to provide background for *Lear* and promised something more rewarding in *Antony and Cleopatra*. When they found they were still to be silent spear-carriers, or the equivalent, a few asked to be released from their contracts. Replacements had to be found, several weeks into rehearsal.

Simon Needs was one who stayed, to understudy several speaking parts and play soldiers and messengers. His reasons were practical: after touring the country in one-off shows, he wanted to be London-based and on a regular income for a while. He had no illusions about 'rising through the ranks' but during his year at the National he would have a chance to work with top actors and directors as well as using the workshop facilities at the NT Studio. When the year was out, a stint at the NT would look good on his curriculum vitae.

In 1987 salaries ranged from about £160 per week (just above the Equity minimum), with a fee per performance of £9, to a top figure of around £450, with a performance fee of £45. The average salary was £250 per week. When negotiating for an actor, Gillian Diamond says she goes purely on theatre track-record, not on work in other media. If an unknown actor comes in to play a lead (as did Jerry Flynn when he did *Golden Boy*) he would get the commensurate basic salary, with a high fee per performance.

Even in the upper echelons, actors are aware that working in the repertoire of either the National or the RSC does not bring fat cheques. In theatre terms, only a West End lead might do that, and television and films (with repeat fees and international buy-outs) are where the big money and widest public – as opposed to artistically prestigious – exposure lies. What they *do* come here for – and are glad to be invited – is a chance to work on the great classical and sometimes obscure plays, which few commercial managements would risk, with some of their finest fellow actors and most experienced directors. They come for the reasons that attracted most of them into the profession in the first place.

CHAPTER 1
Rehearsals Begin
WEEK I Monday 12 January 1987

In the first few days of rehearsal, the intention is to read and talk about the play which, with its 'complex, rich and quite extraordinary language', would, as Hall put it, 'involve them all in an exciting and creative journey'.

The starting point of the journey is the director's decision to do *Antony and Cleopatra* at this particular time, with this particular cast. His own responses to the play, given in his first talk to the company, suggest many of the avenues he intends to explore with them.

'*Antony and Cleopatra*,' he says, 'was Shakespeare's last great tragedy, written in either late 1606 or early 1607, after *Lear* and *Macbeth* and before he moved into the later period of "romances". Playwrights at that time were rather like the early Hollywood screenwriters: unless a work of theirs was very popular, when it would be rushed out in a haphazard Quarto, to make money, it was not considered worth printing.' *Antony and Cleopatra* might have been lost for ever had it not been for the Folio collection of 1623, which was printed after Shakespeare's death, thanks to two fellow actors (and a precedent set by Ben Jonson, ridiculed for gathering the texts of his own plays in a scholarly edition).

The play is based (like *Julius Caesar*, *Coriolanus* and *Timon of Athens*) on North's 1579 translation of a French version of Plutarch's *Life of Marcus Antonius*. 'For both Plutarch and the Elizabethans,' Hall says, 'the purpose of historical biography was ethical: history as a moral example. That great natures can produce great vices as well as great virtues was a perception Plutarch and Shakespeare shared.'

Antony and Cleopatra is a play of action. Quoting Harley Granville Barker, for whom it is 'the most spacious of plays [in which] Shakespeare's eyes swept no wider horizon', Hall reads his crisp summation of the plot and raises a laugh: 'Antony breaks from Cleopatra to patch up an insincere peace with Caesar, since Pompey threatens them both; he marries Octavia and deserts her to return to Cleopatra; war breaks out, Caesar defeats them and they kill themselves.'

The director continues: 'The framework of the play is political: the battle for power within the Roman Empire and the culture clash between expansionist, martial Rome in the West, and Alexandria, sophisticated centre of Greek culture in the East. Every character is concerned about the figure they'll cut on the page of history, what their contemporaries and posterity (noticeably, not God) will think of them. They want to be well-interpreted. Octavius, Antony, Lepidus and Pompey use the sanctions of Roman honour – "The articles of your oath . . .", "The heart of brothers . . . sway our great designs . . .", "If I lose mine honour, I lose myself" – but in practice are ruthless, cold, drunken, two-timing. Self-interest rules. We must investigate the power struggle and hypocrisy.'

(This is a recurring pursuit of Hall's: after doing *The Wars of the Roses* with John Barton at the RSC in 1963, he wrote of his 'fascination with the contortions of politicians and the corrupting seductions experienced by anybody wielding power: I began to collect "sanctions" – those justifications which politicians use in the press or on television to mask the dictates of their party politics or their personal ambitions: "not in the public interest" . . . "I shall do my duty if the country needs me" . . . "let me say quite frankly". . . . What had seemed conventional rhetoric was really . . . an ironic revelation of the time-honoured practices of politicians.')

The centre of the play is what happens when two people fall in love. 'For Shakespeare,' says Hall, 'love was always a madness, a craziness, which led to excess and imbalance (look at the early comedies). *Antony and Cleopatra* is the tragedy of middle-aged people who have loved before and loved often. Realizing that this is perhaps their last opportunity, they savour, revel and bathe in it. Their love possesses them, destroys all rational behaviour. They seem mad, the rest of the world normal.

'Until the nineteenth century, there was no comparable investigation of two people so madly in love that their excesses change one another and change the world itself. Antony and Cleopatra are the most actor-like characters, exhibiting themselves and their power. Displaying the vices of glamorous stars: narcissism, allure, even whoredom, they are both deeply attractive and open to harsh judgement.

'As well as their awfulness, the self-dramatization which is sometimes ridiculous, sometimes stupid, we must always be aware of their greatness, for this is a play about greatness – of lovers, rulers, politicians, who constantly measure themselves against their competitors and for whom there is no use coming second.'

Peter Hall talks at greater length of Shakespeare's idea of order, where anything in excess is wrong. Balance in man leads to balance in society, a weak, self-indulgent ruler will make for a weak, self-indulgent society. In Cleopatra and Antony lack of balance leads to their ruin and makes the world topple: you pay for what you do. Pompey is excessively confident, Octavius extremely rigid. Individual excess is reflected in a world of chaos, civil conflict. Antony's downfall in his thraldom to Cleopatra is mirrored by the decline of the Roman republic during the same period (40 to 30 BC). The Golden Age, of the Romans – and of Elizabeth I – is over.

(This Elizabethan notion of just proportion in all things, is another theme which Hall has continued to explore: 'It is wrong for the heart to rule the head,' he wrote in 1963, 'or for any extremes in persons or politics to be victorious. . . . Working year in and year out on Shakespeare, I began to see this not as a relic of medievalism but as a piece of workable human pragmatism, humanitarian in its philosophy and modern and liberal in its application.')

Antony and Cleopatra has some of the greatest poetry in the language. 'Shakespeare felt absolutely free in his conjoining of words and images; where he is ungrammatical, he fully intends and relishes it so,' says Hall. 'Every character – soldier, attendant, messenger – has a poetic sensibility. . . . The language is almost too rich; it could glut you.' Hall pauses, then adds: 'We are probably living in the last fifty years in which this language is communicable' – an unsettling statement which is to come to mind often in the following weeks.

'The play is highly rhetorical, with the projecting energy of rhetoric, and thus very appropriate to the highly public Olivier Theatre.' Related to this, Hall also stresses the importance he attaches to the correct speaking of the verse, a skill the actors are to acquire so that they maintain a uniformity of style. Here he indicates

Julia Wilson-Dixon, the voice coach: if their voices are in peak condition, they will get so much more out of it.

For background reading, he strongly recommends North's translation of Plutarch and Harley Granville Barker's Preface to *Antony and Cleopatra* (*see Appendix*). Using the latter as a springboard, director and designer are working towards a concept of the classical world as seen through Elizabethan eyes. 'It is difficult to talk about a Shakespearean play: once you are working in it, you realize that each inhabits a very particular world – that of *Antony and Cleopatra* has the warmth, passion and richness of the Renaissance.'

The set is not yet finalized, continues Hall, but will be a big, open space which needs to be filled by people belting on and off, moving the story along. Dominic Muldowney is composing specific music. Problems as yet unresolved include the battles at sea (probably to be done looking out front, with the noise of battle filling the auditorium) and the drawing aloft of Antony into the monument (which, for Hall, has never worked and often seemed ridiculous in previous productions). Since Shakespeare only indicates the divisions between scenes, not acts, in his plays, the appropriate break for an interval is undecided – Hall welcomes all suggestions.

Seated in a circle, the cast goes on to a read-through of the play, which is punctuated by comments from Hall. After the first scene: 'Antony and Cleopatra lead their lives in public. Notice the way in which she winds him up from the beginning. The Ambassadors, newly arrived from Rome, don't know how bad things are: Antony "O'erflows the measure". Both of them are deliberately shown in a bad light.'

After Scene Two, he draws attention to the licence, lightness, wit and femininity of the Egyptian court. The language moves from prose to verse and back again. Charmian and Iras are pretty foul-mouthed. 'If we get the first scenes right, Octavius Caesar should win some sympathy for his moral approbation.' Hall seems clear about the tone he wants to establish for the opening of the play and is laying down tracks for his cast to pursue: 'Excess is the key – whatever you are, be more.'

'In this play, Shakespeare seems to despise the masses and, with our modern-day liberalism, we must avoid the tendency to play this down. Cleopatra has the popular touch, not natural to the Romans who are patrician, stoic, very much a ruling oligarchy. Antony is a champion, a warrior, the embodiment of Hercules: Cleopatra runs rings round him – and he loves it!'

Hall remarks on the pace of the play which is very, very fast until the scenes in which Cleopatra is waiting for Antony, who has returned to Rome. It also slows up for the heavily political scene in which the Triumvirate – Caesar, Lepidus and Antony – are reunited. This is the longest scene thus far, full of irony and undercurrents. That it moves on to Enobarbus' remarkable description of Cleopatra in her barge is a device to keep her at the forefront of our minds and to keep the play spinning along.

Later in the play, Tim Pigott-Smith, in his precise, resonant voice, effortlessly reels off the names of the kings party to Antony and wins a round of applause:

> Bocchus, the King of Libya, Archelaus,
> Of Cappadocia, Philadelphos, King
> Of Paphlagonia, the Thracian King, Adallas,
> King Mauchus of Arabia, King of Pont,
> Herod of Jewry, Mithridates King
> Of Comagene, Polemon and Amyntas,
> The Kings of Mede and Lycaonia . . .

It is rolling, almost biblical language.

An important point made by the director: the three days and nights of battle, mirroring Antony's dissolution, are almost a one-act play within the play. Its shape will have to be clearly defined.

He now gives specific examples of the 'imbalance' he dwelt on in his introductory talk: Antony is the greatest soldier on land. That he risks his reputation by determining to fight at sea at Actium, is due to overweening pride, 'hubris'. Cleopatra's will to remain at the battlefront is 'mannish'. (It is noteworthy that all the fighting in this play occurs offstage.)

After the defeat of Actium, Antony sits on the ground in despair (a move actually given by Shakespeare in the First Folio). Cleopatra comes in and she, too, sinks to the floor. There is no question but that this scene will be built on the distinct image of two larger-than-life beings on the ground, apart, with their attendants trying to bring them together.

Cleopatra cannot help flirting with, charming, every man she meets (including Caesar's Ambassador); it is part of her armoury as a survivor. We should understand Enobarbus' growing determination to desert Antony, whose actions must appear increasingly self-destructive and unbalanced.

Act V, the final section of the play, after Antony's death, is (in Hall's words) 'as though half the world has gone'. The new tension of the play is Cleopatra pitted against Octavius Caesar – a Caesar already envisaging his memoirs, planning the most favourable end to this Egyptian business and his triumphal return to Rome.

This first read-through, which has taken a day and a half, with stops for discussion, has given some idea of the monumental scale of the play, and the pacing and flow within it. Scenes are, in the main, brief and cut back and forth: from Alexandria, to Rome, back to Egypt, to another part of Italy (where Pompey is encamped), to Parthia, to Athens. The effect is cinematographic – and somewhat overwhelming.

Much later on, Hall is to say that he had no particular vision of the play when he started – to have had one would, he feels, have been limiting. Yet with hindsight I can say that, in his first talk to his actors, and in his comments during their first read-through, he prepared the ground for virtually everything that was to be fleshed out, in dramatic terms, in the weeks ahead. His insights came from an almost religious attention to the text, its clues and signposts.

CHAPTER 2

Blocking the Play – and Telling its Story

WEEKS 1 and 2

Before rehearsals began, I was given an outline of the way in which Peter Hall would use the allotted time:

Weeks 1, 2 & 3   – discussion and plotting of movement

Weeks 4, 5, 6 & 7 – the 'meat' of the piece, getting to grips with emotional and intellectual detail

Weeks 8, 9 & 10 – a period of reassessment

Weeks 11 & 12   – radical re-staging and finalizing of all technicalities

Week 13   – public previews and press nights

As I look at the period in retrospect, these stages were indeed gone through. At the time, however, there was a sense in which they occurred concurrently: reassessment took place from day to day, scenes were restaged as the thinking behind them altered, the appropriate movement for a particular piece of business might only reveal itself in the tenth week. Scenes were run and re-run with accumulating insight. A run-through (of an Act or the entire play) allows for a periodic check on how the segments are locking together and on how the narrative line has been modulated. The image, for me, is of a giant carousel, which became more sharply focused, more intensely coloured, with each revolution. The rehearsal process is a rolling stone which does gather moss, layers and layers of it.

In French, the word for rehearsal is *répétition*. Innumerable ideas are generated in the course of a day's work; as well as being intellectually understood, these ideas must become emotionally convincing if they are to communicate and it is the constant repetition of rehearsing that scores them deep into the actors' psyche so that, by the time of eventual performance, there is a rich vein of the subconscious to be tapped and responses have become largely instinctive. This happens to the extent that, after an electrifying performance, an actor will often not know what he did exactly: it is as if he had gone into automatic gear.

In answer to the invariable question: 'How do they remember all the words?', that too is a function of repetition. Going over the lines of the script again and again in rehearsal, in association with a repeated pattern of movement and an increasingly familiar physical context, whole chunks of the text are absorbed almost effortlessly, whilst consciously learned lines become ingrained.

Midway through the first week, Peter Hall and the cast start plotting, or blocking, the play, lifting it off the page into action. Hall comes as if to an open canvas, his script free of preconceived moves.

In Rehearsal Room 3 there are charts on the walls: a map of the Mediterranean from 800 BC and a genealogy of the Caesars and Ptolemies. A scene-by-scene breakdown of the play, with actors listed alongside, cross-references each scene they are in and the character they play in it. This is particularly helpful to many of them 'doubling' in several parts. From it, too, stage management can work out the daily rehearsal calls, a minefield of complexity.

The rehearsal room is well heated. Outside, the temperature is below freezing, trains are not running, roads are deep in snow.

Alison Chitty, the National's only resident designer, works from an office-cum-workspace on the fourth floor. The first time she worked with Peter Hall was on *Martine*, with its memorable evocation of poppies and cornfields stretching to the horizon. Designs created for the RSC include a perspective railway carriage for Stephen Poliakoff's *Breaking the Silence*, and she was working with Hall towards the opening of the latest Poliakoff, *Coming in to Land*, only four days before *Antony and Cleopatra* went into rehearsal.

Normally, a production meeting involving the director and all those dealing with the physical aspects of a production (set and costume, lighting and sound designers, production and stage management), along with someone from the finance department, is held before rehearsals begin, to talk through the schedule of construction, anticipate likely problems and deal with the financial constraints. Because *Antony and Cleopatra*, however, followed so closely on the heels of *Coming in to Land*, this assembly splintered into a series of mini-meetings and phone-calls between individuals.

Usually, too, costume designs, a model of the set and floor plans are shown to the cast on the first day of rehearsal. Before they can start to feel their way towards the movement suggested by the text, the actors need to know the physical context within which they will be working.

Designer and director had discussed six or seven possible ways of staging *Antony and Cleopatra*, all incorporating circles and domes to create a sense of the world and sky, and related to the Olivier Theatre context. Inspired by the Harley Granville Barker essay, they have come up with the final concept for the set just as the play goes into rehearsal. Working under pressure, Chitty then has to translate this concept into a physical reality before blocking begins.

She arrives in the rehearsal room with a model of the set, places it on a table and everyone crowds round. Built to scale, it reveals the result in miniature: against a deep maroon cyclorama,* on a rounded floor area, stands an inner semi-circle. This is made up of three sections – two curved side walls and a central set of doors, pillared and pedimented – each of which can retreat or advance along floor-tracks, separately or together, to form varying configurations.

'The big problem with the Olivier Theatre is to govern the space,' says Hall. By echoing the circle of the stage, they have created a containing framework for the action – one that will 'hold' the space so that the actors are strengthened, not diminished, by its vastness. The other priority was to make this space elastic, so that it could move rapidly from the domestic to the universal and back again – hence the mobile walls and doors, which can close in for intimate scenes and pull back so that processions and armies marching use the outer circles of the stage.

'It's fair to say that the design of this production is as much "work in progress" as our rehearsals,' advises Hall. 'We want to create a hot, sensuous space which can be both classical and Egyptian. The Roman colours are cool, the Egyptian, heated, sexy, sun-filled. . . .'

'We will have a problem clarifying when we are in Egypt, when in Rome, but costumes, props and lighting will help,' adds Chitty. 'I

---

* A curved curtain or screen at the back of the stage, concealing rear-wall, scene 'docks', actors waiting to make an entrance etc.

want to get the effect of a corner of a Renaissance painting, with a glimpse of ruins, light and shadow in folds of material. . . .'

She speaks intently, referring to the model to illustrate the points she is making: 'For the scene on Pompey's galley everyone will sit at a long central table facing the audience. It's an image from da Vinci's *Last Supper*, just as Antony's being lowered into the monument is curiously like a Renaissance image of the Deposition of Christ. The costumes will not be historical Egyptian or Roman but Renaissance, with suggestions of both, as in the paintings of Mantegna, Veronese and Titian.' (This, too, has come from Granville Barker's writing.)

Chitty's brown eyes scan the encircling actors: 'I'd like to get a photographer in to record each of your faces and shapes.' She shows several plates from a volume on Mantegna's *Triumphs of Caesar*: 'Look, each figure is an individual, drawn from life.' These Mantegnas will provide details of battle tunics, helmets, shields and spectacular Roman standards and banners. As source material and fuel for her imagination, she will also draw on Rubens ('for the emotion'), books on Egypt after the Pharaohs, Roman portraits, and the work of such Orientalists as the Victorian David Roberts (depicting tiny, robed and turbaned figures dwarfed by temples along the Nile). She is adamant about not being an academic: authenticity of sets and costumes is subjugated to the interests of telling the story as clearly as possible. She works through intuition.

The focus now turns to the rehearsal area itself. A tall set of unpainted wooden doors and two calico screens, all on castors, represent the movable sections of the set. On the floor, a large semicircle in white tape – with spaces to mark the three aisles into the auditorium – outlines half the area of the Olivier stage. (Once they move into the immense cavern of Rehearsal Room 1, in a week's time, it will be possible to tape out the full circle.) Converging diagonals of green tape are a guide to the movement of the walls and there is a red perpendicular along which the central doors will move back and forwards.

The stage managers have assembled an assortment of props and furniture: stools, benches, carved chairs, rugs, floor cushions, flagons and heavy wine goblets. More will be added as the play progresses – swords, shields, halberds, and tall, tasselled banners – first recycled from past productions, later to be replaced by those made in the workshops to Alison Chitty's design.

Just before they move out on to the floor, Peter Hall says something which he is to reiterate throughout rehearsals – and which is a feature of all his Shakespearean productions: 'Remember that the central space is an Elizabethan space, always filled, one scene rapidly giving way to another, overlapping. There will *not* be hold-ups as scenery trundles back and forth. . . .'

Act I Scene 1. The play opens: Demetrius (Brian Spink) and Philo (Mike Hayward), Roman emissaries to the court of Alexandria, make an energetic entrance through the doors, followed soon after by Cleopatra and Antony, Charmian and Iras, who circle the stage.

Hall: 'Should the eunuchs be backing before them, fanning?' Alan Cohen: 'Petals being strewn . . .?' Judi Dench: 'It's as if they're behaving very badly in public, shoddily.' Hall: 'It's all jokes and wine and staying up all night.' Hopkins: 'Why and where are they progressing?' Hall: 'To or from a meal, as though you're going off to your private chambers. Weave an Eastern, joyous, sexy spell upon the space.' (He indicates the shape on a floor-plan pinned up on the wall.) 'What binds Antony and Cleopatra is over-riding lust. I don't mean that they don't like each other, but she's never the same for five minutes, changeable, quixotic, difficult. They have constant conflicts. He's a bit of a masochist.'

So images, ambiance and attitudes rapidly accrue: in order to find the logic for what happens onstage, the actors must create a sense of life beyond the visible arena. Everything vibrates round that central relationship. Before Antony and Cleopatra enter, the text prepares us for 'a gypsy' and 'a strumpet's fool'; the opening procession provides them with a superbly theatrical opportunity to display that lust of which Hall spoke and to establish an Egyptian court suffused with it. (He quotes the remark of a Victorian who saw the play: 'How unlike the home life of our own dear Queen!')

Much of the blocking period involves determining the story of each scene. Of course, this is dependent on interpretation by a particular director and cast, at a particular time and in a particular place – there is no 'pure' version. For example, in his Preface to *Antony and Cleopatra*, Harley Granville Barker is at pains to convince us that, because Shakespeare's Cleopatra would have been acted by a boy and the 'sensual charm which drew Antony to her' could therefore only have been shown 'objectionably or ridiculously', the playwright has studiously avoided any scene in which she and Antony physically interact. Although a supreme man of the theatre, he was also a man of his – Edwardian – times. *He* reads 'sensuality sublimated' into the opening scene, where Hall – working in the 1980s – sees evidence in the text for behaviour which overtly provokes the watching Romans. Otherwise hugely in sympathy, both directors are influenced by the mores of their era.

In Act I Scene 2, white-haired Daniel Thorndike plays the Soothsayer. From him, the director wants 'neutrality and superiority – the Delphic oracle'. With Miranda Foster, he works on making Charmian's three wishes distinct, the key words clearly etched: 'Let me be *married* to three *kings* in a forenoon and *widow* them *all*./Let me have a *child* at *fifty* to whom *Herod of Jewry* may do *homage*./Find me to *marry* me with *Octavius Caesar*, and companion *me* with my *mistress*.'

They try it down on the floor, on cushions. Then the wider world impinges on this hothouse of the senses: Antony has agreed to hear Demetrius, the Messenger from Rome. The Empire is under threat: in Italy itself his wife Fulvia and his brother have made war against Antony's fellow-Triumvir, Octavius Caesar, and the Parthians are encroaching on its eastern boundaries. Further news (its shock value framed in the menacing sibilance of the place-name 'Sicyon', thrice repeated, as Hall points out) is that Fulvia is dead. Antony realizes that he and his forces must return to Rome, but Enobarbus takes some convincing that they are really going – he is still caught up in the enchantment of Egypt and its passionate queen who 'catching but the least noise of this, dies instantly'. So we, the audience, are made to anticipate her reactions to the news. We also get the first mention of another factor which endangers peace in Italy – Sextus Pompeius (Pompey) and his command of the sea.

During the lunchbreak, in the theatre canteen overlooking the Thames, Anthony Hopkins is refuelling (sausages and beans) and considering his role.

Currently alternating between feelings of intense depression and elation, depending on his most recent performance as Lear, he has not yet felt free to concentrate on Antony. Hall has told him not to be concerned: all the right qualities are there, it will come . . .

Hopkins is fascinated by such people of monumental talent as

Judy Garland, Orson Wells and Richard Burton; as if cursed by an urge for self-destruction, they burned themselves out in excess or addiction. It is a mis-channelling of energy the actor knows well and speaks of with exhilaration, having surmounted his own alcoholism. Autobiography feeds interpretation and it is with a sense of 'Eureka!' that he goes back to rehearse: 'Antony is always in his cups, unable to resist any pleasure, addicted to Cleopatra – and to drink.'

Act I Scene 3, the scene in which Antony has to break the news of his imminent departure to a raging and heartsore Cleopatra, involves everyone in a discussion about the contrast in their behaviour when they are together and when they are apart. In the midst of a polite, fawning court, they are excessive and parading, larger than life. She can be cruel, vulgar, perverse, emotional, animal. It is only when away from him that she can reveal her vulnerability and fear of ageing. To her confidantes she is not reticent about her past loves and the fact that she is on the cusp of middle age.

Hopkins, fired by his notion of Antony as 'a bit of a lush', thinks Cleopatra would probably have seen him in a drunken stupor, vomiting. But when she is not around (as in the preceding scene, when he dealt with the news from Rome) we should see the power of the great warrior and politician.

Act I Scene 4 is the first scene between Octavius Caesar (Tim Pigott-Smith) and Lepidus (John Bluthal) with their advisors – Agrippa (Basil Henson) and Maecenas (Graham Sinclair).

Moving in to decide the overlap with the previous scene, Hall uses film technology to make his favourite point: 'In the best times I've ever had with Shakespeare there were none of those messy dissolves, the stage never went cold.'

A boardroom-type table is introduced, with several imposing high-backed chairs. One is noticeably vacant: Caesar is enraged by Antony's continuing absence in Egypt, whilst Pompey and his pirates threaten Rome:

Antony

Leave thy lascivious wassails . . .

Hall comments on Caesar's corrosive quality, his extraordinary breaks into bitterness – or lyricism – when he is in the midst of stating facts.

Act I Scene 5. Blocking continues with the first scene in which

Cleopatra awaits news of Antony. The women start to work in long calico skirts, brought down from the wardrobe. A rug and several floor-cushions are placed downstage for them to recline on. Alexas (Robert Arnold) delivers a message and a gift from Antony.

Judi Dench, of Cleopatra: 'She's desolate, restless – that's how you get in the East when your fella's away. . . . All I've had is one airmail letter and an orient pearl!' Later, after Charmian has teased Cleopatra about her past love for Julius Caesar: 'She turns everything to her advantage. . . . One minute Charmian and Iras feel secure enough to be quite cheeky, the next – pow! – she's slapping them round the room. She's quite capable of "unpeopling Egypt" of killing one of her own followers, of killing herself. . . .'

Act II Scene 1. The story (from Peter Hall): Pompey comes in, with sidekicks Menas and Menecrates, pirates, almost as a Hitler-figure, presenting himself to a cheering populace – 'I'm going to be the victor, bigger than my father (Pompey the Great), stronger than Caesar or Antony.' Alison Chitty: 'I see you all weather- and weapon-proofed, perhaps in leather, whatever makes the most powerful effect.'

Where another director might have decided on an inward-turning war conference, Hall introduces a confrontational device – Pompey acknowledging mass acclaim at a rally – using the evidence of the bombastic language:

> I shall do well.
> The people love me and the sea is mine;
> My powers are crescent and my auguring hope
> Says it will come to th' full. . . .

David Schofield comes on, bullishly powerful as Pompey. Hall immediately interposes with the verse, its pointing and scansion. Schofield, Roman-profiled Peter Gordon (Menas) and tall Michael Carter (Menecrates) suggest that they assemble weapons and polish armour to underline their preparation for war. The screens, moved in, create a feeling of menace, as of a powder keg about to explode.

Act II Scene 2. The first encounter between Caesar and Antony (entering from opposite sides of the stage) with Lepidus as intermediary. The conference table and chairs are brought on again.

Peter Hall: 'It's like a summit meeting: you see them all smiling and courteous but there's danger in the air. Politicians use truth and candour as calculatedly as they use lies.' (As the leading figure in British theatre, an outspoken protagonist in the fight for government funding of the arts, and the subject of much media attention, he speaks wrily, with an insider's knowledge of the political arena.) 'Antony uses openness and ingenuousness to achieve his ends,' he continues. 'It's only because things go badly that he agrees to marry Octavia, Caesar's sister.'

Tim Pigott-Smith feels sure that Caesar is taken aback when the marriage is suggested, that (as later scenes show) he has genuine feelings for his sister, and is not cold-bloodedly using her, as a pawn in the political game.

When the leaders depart, Enobarbus, Agrippa and Maecenas relax into the chairs they have vacated. Michael Bryant lolls back, his feet propped up on the conference table. He delivers the breathtakingly beautiful description of Cleopatra in her barge thoughtfully and without embellishment, so that each image shimmers and is yet very concrete. The actor has had to decide why Shakespeare put poetry of such lyricism into the mouth of a cynic – and how to put it across credibly: he makes it the old campaigner talking to his friends, conjuring up memories over which he chuckles in nostalgic wonder:

> . . . . She did lie
> In her pavilion, cloth-of-gold of tissue,
> O'erpicturing that Venus where we see
> The fancy outwork nature. On each side her
> Stood pretty dimpled boys like smiling cupids, . . .
> . . . . At the helm
> A seeming mermaid steers. The silken tackle
> Swell with the touches of those flower-soft hands
> That yarely frame the office.

and:

> . . . . Our courteous Antony
> Whom ne'er the word of 'no' woman heard speak
> Being barbered ten times o'er, goes to the feast
> And, for his ordinary, pays his heart
> For what his eyes eat only.

Challenged by Hall: 'What do you think of Cleopatra?', Bryant thinks, says: 'He's captured – in love with her, I suppose.' 'And of Octavia?' To which Basil Henson replies drily: 'Well, she's clean . . .

a good cook. . . .' The truth is that a marriage between Antony and Octavia will not last. He will be drawn like a magnet back to Cleopatra who 'makes hungry where most she satisfies' and whom 'age cannot wither'.

Act II Scene 3. Enobarbus' foreboding is soon given substance: when Antony and Octavia meet, under Caesar's watchful eye, Antony at first seems sincere, promising her that 'that to come/Shall all be done by th' rule'. But once she and her brother have gone and the Soothsayer emerges, warning 'hie you to Egypt again. . . . Thy lustre thickens when he [Caesar] shines by', Antony does not need much persuasion. By the end of the scene he is determined to return to Cleopatra – and is sending Ventidius to fight the Parthians, rather than assuming the responsibility himself.

Act II Scene 4. A scene 'en passant': the marriage with Octavia having been effected, Agrippa and Maecenas are on their way to the confrontation with Pompey. Hall stages it as one long diagonal of movement, from upstage right to downstage left. The 'choreography' gives a sense of urgency and literally drives the action forward.

Act II Scene 5 returns the play to Egypt. A Messenger brings Cleopatra the news of Antony's marriage, to which she reacts with a mixture of fury and anguish. Jerry Flynn (Eros), small and slight, starts off diffidently but comes into his own when he shows Judi Dench how to 'hale him up and down', dragging him across the floor by his hair (which, in fact, he holds, she gripping his hand). The physicality releases him.

Act II Scene 6. Assembled for battle against Pompey, the Triumvirate confront him with their peace offer: he is to rid the sea of pirates, in exchange for Sicily and Sardinia.

'David,' says Hall, 'they have made you an offer you can't refuse, but you are full of historic grievances and if you can break up the Triumvirate, you'd be delighted. So you're stirring things up, chipping away at Antony with your references to Egypt.'

The four contenders circle round one another, physically expressing the political undercurrents. Antony, in bravado, declares, 'We'll speak with thee at sea' and Lepidus and Caesar move in to block him and placate Pompey. Standing apart, a gruff bulldog in defence of his master Antony, Enobarbus cuts in on the verbal fencing. According to Hall, he is 'the man Shakespeare loves, blunt, honest, without guile'. Even at this early stage in rehearsals, Bryant's accent has thickened, his vocal tone come down, echoed by the simplicity and characteristic lack of posturing of the actor's stance.

How to create the imagery of imminent war? With banners, fanfares? 'Let's have four trumpeters on stage. We can back it up electronically,' declares Hall, who hates these scenes of armies confronting one another. 'I mean, the language and characters are interesting, but there's no movement. Let's take the space, open it right out.' They do, and it is at once more theatrical, more dangerous.

Act II Scene 7. Hall consults his designer and actors about the banquet of reconciliation on Pompey's galley. To create Chitty's *Last Supper* image, three trestles make up a long table facing the audience, with stools positioned along the upstage side. The scene will be 'held' by two walls of ropes, dropped on pulleys ('flown in') from above the stage and clipped to the floor or wall sections on either side. There will be flagons of wine and bowls of something which can be scooped up by hand (pasta? a seafood risotto?). Emma Lloyd, stage manager responsible for props, makes a note.

Dramatically, the director calls for an image of excess: 'As if, after Yalta, Stalin is stuffed with food, Churchill reeling about. Then we get travellers' tales, of the Nile, "pyramises", "strange serpents", crocodiles. It's a parody of the mystique of Egypt. The dance should be grotesque. The pure and exquisite Boy's song makes everyone feel maudlin.'

Act III Scene 1. Ventidius, having been dispatched to Parthia by Antony, has won a great victory. The body of Pacorus, the defeated king's son, is born in on a stretcher. Alan Cohen makes a note for music and sound: triumphal fanfares and cheering. Hall points out Shakespeare's purposeful juxtaposition of this scene with the previous one.

> Caesar and Antony have ever won
> More in their officer than person . . .

Ventidius explains to fellow officer Silius that he fears to pursue his Parthian conquests lest he outdo and thereby offend Antony. The twofold function of this scene is to show a man undergoing the dangers his leader has avoided, and the tactical risks of working for Antony who, despite his magnanimity and charm, is part of the ruthless, power-crazed world in which the play is set. Peter Hall wants a lot of character, presence and colour: 'Not just two boring old soldiers in the aftermath of battle. We'll surround you with banners and bloodied, wounded men.'

In these initial weeks, the structure of the play is being investigated: why is this scene placed here? What does it reveal about the characters? How is the story being furthered? Ferreting meaning out of complex lines, making connections and tracing the throughline of the narrative, the actors are well embarked upon the 'exciting and creative journey' of which Hall spoke.

Act III Scene 2. Antony has command of the eastern portion of the Empire. Octavia is about to go off with him 'to be an army wife' (as Basil Henson says). She and Caesar are reluctant to part and, as she is led in between brother and husband, her distress makes her seem physically torn between the two.

Hall points out a curious reversal of our preconceptions. 'The Romans of that time were supposed to be stoic: it is a religion for Agrippa and Maecenas, and Caesar is control itself overall. Remember, though, that until the time of Wellington – when the whole "stiff upper lip" thing came in – the English were emotional, and showy about it and it is the *Elizabethan* in Octavia and Caesar which breaks through – and is always there in Antony, the man of greatest passion. This is a scene about attempting to suppress emotion. It emerges in Octavia's surprising weeping.'

Wanting emotion beneath containment, Hall has deliberately cast exuberant Sally Dexter as Octavia, the woman described as being 'of a holy, cold and still conversation'. 'If the audience were asked, at the end of this scene, if Antony was going back to Cleopatra, they should be unsure,' contends Hall. 'He really seems to be making an effort, touched by his wife's vulnerability, sincere in his warmth and friendship to Caesar, his new brother-in-law.'

At every opportunity, Hall draws attention to language: 'Note that whenever anything is ominous or is deeply felt, Shakespeare breaks into verse . . . Watch how emotion is forced under control by prose, or by verse which is full of jagged, angular words, divested of poetic images. The weight of a line, its sense, is almost always in the second half.' Dexter has never done Shakespeare before and is learning to carry the verse alongside the sense. She compares this to working on a musical, 'looking for the rhythm and the melody, the major and secondary themes'.

Act III Scene 3. Again, we are in Egypt. Dench is deliciously funny, reading from her script, as she cross-examines the Messenger whom she had previously attacked, about Octavia: Is she as tall as me? what does she sound like? look like? How old is she? She distorts each reply to reassure herself that Antony 'cannot like her long'. Cleopatra's entourage form an anxious semi-circle behind her as she makes darting forays towards the nervous young man trapped downstage left.

Act III Scene 4 returns us to Antony and his new wife, now in Athens. The relationship between Octavia's husband and her brother has already begun to sour, tearing at her dual loyalties. Antony's desire to be back with Cleopatra is an undercurrent; unable to look her in the eye, he keeps his distance from Octavia. The pugilistic set of Hopkins' shoulders, the defiant jut of his beard, present her with an impenetrable barrier. Hall summarizes: 'This scene is here to show us that whatever fantasy Antony had, of behaving and toeing the line, is now gone.'

Act III Scene 5. In a world where news is passed on by gossip and rumour, Eros tells Enobarbus that 'a third of the world' is now deposed: Lepidus is under house arrest. This is momentous; the field is now left to Antony and Caesar.

(Jerry Flynn is doubling as Eros, Antony's batman, as well as playing the Messenger bearing news of Antony's marriage. With satisfying logic, he had suggested making a single character of the two roles.)

Hall: 'Notice that Shakespeare does not dramatize the break-up of the Triumvirate. Instead, we get Eros describing Antony's reactions to it. . . . Jerry, you're treating it a bit too literally. It's prose with the formality of verse, full of assonance and consonance. Invest the words with a little more consciousness. Savour them:

. . . . would not let him partake in the glory of the action and,
(breath) not resting here, *(a springboard)* accuses him of letters he
had formerly wrote to Pompey.

'Don't put in punctuation which isn't there, even in prose.'

Act III Scene 6 is fuelled by Caesar's rage: Antony has set himself up as a king in Alexandria, given his kingdom away to Cleopatra, their 'unlawful issue', and to Caesarion (her son by Julius Caesar). When Octavia arrives from Athens, unheralded, not even aware that

Antony has returned to Cleopatra, Tim Pigott-Smith gives vent to a
terrific steam of anger, whilst she stands immobile:

> . . . . The wife of Antony
> Should have an army for an usher and
> The neighs of horses to tell of her approach
> Long ere she did appear. The trees by th'way
> Should have borne men and expectation fainted,
> . . . . But you are come
> A market maid to Rome. . . .

Hall is delighted: 'This speech has always worried me. It's so high-
flown. As rage, it works, and accounts for the hyperbole of the
language.'

The actor jokes: 'I didn't even have time to crucify a few Christians
for her.' Although initially directed at Octavia, his anger arises from
pain – and pity – on her behalf. As Caesar, Pigott-Smith's emotion
has a repressed quality: his shoulders and elbows draw in, his fists
tighten, movement is robot-like and spasmodic.

The scene is plotted first with Octavia creeping in from stage left.
Then it is restaged: self-possessed and staunch, she enters upstage
and walks forward into the midst of her brother and his supporters,
creating confusion amongst them, and giving the scene definition
and impact.

Act III Scene 7 starts with Cleopatra haranguing Enobarbus for
saying that it is not fitting that a woman participate in the coming
wars against Caesar:

> And as president of my kingdom will
> Appear there for a man.

Then she backs Antony's decision to fight by sea, at which he is not
skilled. (Hall points out the contrast between her assertiveness and
Octavia's dutiful acceptance of her brother's 'Pray you, Be ever
known to patience' in the previous scene.)

Dench is brisk and businesslike, Hopkins more cautious, needing
background information about where they are, how news has arrived
about Caesar's advance, how much advice he would take from his
generals. In this scene, Bryant's Enobarbus is very much the veteran, bluntly warning his captain about the dangers of throwing
away 'The absolute soldiership you have by land'. Dan Thorndike,

seasoned actor, doubles as the seasoned general Canidius (a contrast to his Soothsayer role).

Actors and director concentrate on meaning and motives, staging is left open, with the main protagonists centre-stage, the others grouped round them.

For Act III Scenes 8 and 9, Peter Hall and Alan Cohen discuss the back-up of soldiers required: they will need to muster as large an army as possible, perhaps to include ushers and usherettes.

Act III Scene 10. The progress of the battle of Actium is reported by Enobarbus and Scarus (Andrew Wadsworth), as they look out front, supposedly towards the sea. 'I never saw an action of such shame', says Scarus, describing how Antony, 'like a doting mallard', left the battle at its height, to sail after a fleeing Cleopatra. Canidius enters: he is about to turn himself over to Caesar:

> O he has given example for our flight
> Most grossly by his own.

Act III Scene 11. Antony's humiliation after the defeat of Actium. He drives away his remaining followers and then sits, as if his shame is insupportable. On the opposite side of the stage, Cleopatra sits too, overwhelmed by what she has caused. This was the image indelible from the first read-through. Charmian, Iras, Mardian and Eros hover and finally get her to approach him. 'Antony is the arch seducer of all time,' muses Hall:

> Fall not a tear I say, one of them rates
> All that is won and lost. Give me a kiss.
> Even this repays me.

They continue to block the play to the end, looking for movement and grouping which illuminate the text. Mined intelligently, it really does provide directives for playing each scene, in terms of action (or indeed, stillness), use (or non-use) of furniture and props, and placing of the set. Nothing should be extraneous or contradictory; all should combine to propel the play forwards.

Sometimes the exploration in these early weeks hits an intensity never reached again. The precision achieved by instinct can be diluted by the uncovery of too many choices, the busy-ness of subsequent rehearsals.

When they arrive at the scene in which Eros kills himself and

Antony attempts the same, movement is minimal. The two actors stand reading, releasing thought and feeling line by line:

> ANTONY   Sometime we see a cloud that's dragonish,
> A vapour sometime like a bear or lion . . .
> . . . . Thou hast seen these signs;
> They are black vesper's pageants.
>
> EROS   Ay my lord.
>
> ANTONY   That which is a horse, even with a thought
> The rack dislimns and makes it indistinct
> As water is in water.
>
> EROS   It does my lord.
>
> ANTONY   My good knave Eros, now thy captain is
> Even such a body. Here I am Antony
> Yet cannot hold this visible shape, my knave.

The skill is to capture the moment and perpetuate it.

As Hall had said, Alison Chitty's design for this production is 'work in progress': partly through circumstance, partly by intent, the design is *following* the rehearsal process and incorporating ideas to which the actors are party. Creatively satisfying for everyone in the rehearsal room, it will certainly put an added pressure on the construction schedule.

A high platform and a flight of stairs, both on castors, have been brought in to represent the monument in which Cleopatra takes refuge. Although details for this are not finalized, we are told that it will telescope out of the central door structure, with Antony being hauled aloft by a pulley projecting from it.

There is discussion about how Cleopatra can be captured from up in the monument, to play out her last scenes on the stage below. Hall: 'Manhandling you down will be good.' Judi Dench: 'Marvellous! Think what it will do to her dignity!' (and this after she has been told there is a fifteen-foot drop).

After talking through the projected complications of her death – throne to be brought on (when and where?), elaborate robe and mantle to be donned, live snakes . . . they finally arrive at Caesar's funeral oration: and invention runs dry.

Now that it is being staged *Antony and Cleopatra* seems even more overwhelming than at the read-through. Peter Hall had mentioned that there is a myth of impossibility attached to it: having just spoken to Peggy Ashcroft (whose acclaimed Cleopatra was thirty-five years before) he repeats her words: 'You know you'll never get there, but it's quite clear where you're going.'

End of WEEK 2 – DAY 10 – Friday 23 January

Four floors above the workshops and Rehearsal Room 1, in an office filled with light, plants and architectural drawings, is Michael Cass-Jones (Cass), Production Manager for all the plays going into the Olivier Theatre. It is his job to co-ordinate construction of each set, and to supervise the stage staff who will eventually handle it.

In theory, during the countdown period leading to the first public preview, he should have:

Outline designs	at 18 weeks before
Final design/scale-model/agreed budget	at 16 weeks
Working drawings	at 14 weeks

This leaves 4 weeks in which to plan and purchase materials and 10 for workshop construction. Yet, with 11 weeks to go before *Antony and Cleopatra* opens, discussion is still under way about the movable sections of the set and whether the financial parameters will allow for the required degree of Renaissance lavishness. Cass-Jones seems unperturbed; his main concern is *Six Characters in Search of an Author*, due to open next in the Olivier.

He reminds me that Alison Chitty would have had to keep in mind the constraints of the National's repertoire system, as she was turning the concept for her set into a workable reality: in a two-hour changeover, the set of one production must be got out, that of *Antony and Cleopatra* got in, lighting re-angled and checked.

In Chitty's office nearby, her assistant David Neat is researching designs for a funeral bier (for the scene in Parthia), a weapon rack (to be used by Pompey's men) and an Egyptian throne which will both look right and be practical (so that Cleopatra can be carried offstage in it).

Down in the rehearsal room, after lunch, the blocking complete, the play is to have a first run-through.

Peter Hall stands or sits behind a lectern, on which his script lies open, centred to the stage area. Alan Cohen is at a table alongside.

Stage management tables for Ernie Hall, Emma Lloyd and Angie Bissett are near the rehearsal room door and telephone (with incoming calls 'flashed' rather than rung). Paul Greaves sits in a large carved chair, before an ornate desk on the other side of the room; in front of him, propped-up prompt script, reading lamp, note pads, vases of flowers (real and artificial) and a bowl containing a constant supply of sweets for the company. As prompter, he hardly budges from that desk for the duration of rehearsals.

As Hall explains, the forthcoming run is to get the flow of the narrative, to find out how one scene connects with the next. He asks his cast not for 'acting' but for thought. Yet, when they start, there is a feeling of rising to the occasion, the tension of 'getting it right'. Ernie Hall calls 'House lights down . . .Action!' and they are off.

It is obvious that a lot of homework has been done, despite the demands of other productions (in the past ten days, for instance, Bryant has done seven performances of *Lear* and three of *American Clock* – which, after a fortnight out of the repertoire, needed a word-run to warm it up, as well as several cast-replacement rehearsals).

These actors are well-honed. Their voices in good condition, speech crisp, bodies both relaxed and primed. They project energy. Anthony Hopkins alone has taken Hall at his word, and, resisting the pressure to 'perform', is prowling his way introspectively through the words. The pace, generally, slows and settles.

The first confrontation between Antony and Caesar feels good: the pauses are given weight, the thought process and nuances of subtext come across. Already Tim Pigott-Smith only needs to glance at his script for reference. Playing various Messengers, Michael Bottle has been grappling with the scansion: he suddenly finds the sense in the metre.

Stage Management are excellent, alert to one another, making it possible for each scene to flow into the next. Emma Lloyd, on props, gets tables, stools and state chairs on and off and moves the doors and side-screens forward and back, helped by two young actors whom she briefs between scenes.

Paul Greaves has been marking up the prompt script for use during performances, with pauses which, by being repeated, are becoming fixed. He also keeps an eye on the actors' entrances, exits and positions on stage, to amend them in his script as rehearsals progress. Ernie Hall times the run. All the while Alison Chitty is making notes and sketching, especially during the grouping of the soldiers.

Peter Hall has been completely fixated on the script, immobile, the usual post-prandial cigar not in evidence. Afterwards, expressing deep satisfaction ('the whole thing looks very healthy. We have a wonderful company to do a stupendous play') he reiterates the need to keep the stage 'always possessed, never empty or dead': he is aiming for a vigorous overlap of scene upon scene. He will also have to orchestrate 'a lot of running about of as many soldiers as possible': actors and stage management will be interchanging emblematic banners, standards and shields to denote the different armies in this 'civil war'. And the placing of the interval is still a problem: 'where to put it without raping the muscles of the play and the way in which they interact' (Hall). An audience begins to get restless at 1 hour 25 minutes. . . .

Chitty is now clear that she is aiming for a look, in costumes and wigs, which is 'classical on the outside, Renaissance internally'. For Alan Cohen 'we need to rationalize the space', to pinpoint the function of the various door and wall configurations. (This operates on two levels: providing a sense of geography – a battle plain, the court in Egypt – as well as a feeling of enclosure or exposure.)

This first run-through takes 3 hours 55 minutes, with the inclusion of unavoidable hitches. Given the intentional looseness of the plotting period, I am frankly amazed at the extent to which things come together. Beneath the informality of rehearsals, the endless anecdotes and laughter, there is a grip of absolute professionalism.

CHAPTER 3

Language: 'Content and Structure are Indivisible'

WEEK 3 – Monday 26 January

There is a chapter in Simon Callow's book, *Being an Actor*, in which he describes his marathon delivery of Shakespeare's 148 sonnets ('More verse than the roles of Hamlet, Lear and Othello put together'), in Platform Performance at the National. Afterwards, Peter Hall suggested he could make him 'not just a very fine verse speaker but one of the best in the country'. The sessions that followed were to be a revelation for Callow, leading him to feel that 'the couple of hours that I spent with Peter Hall should be available to all actors in some form'.

Hall himself has said that his proudest achievement is to have brought back a standard of speaking and understanding Shakespeare by actors. During the first weeks of rehearsal of *Antony and Cleopatra*, he constantly drew attention to the form of the verse, urging the actors to find and keep to the iambic pentameter whilst they investigated the meaning of the lines.

Thus they were already primed for a talk on the handling of Shakespearean verse, with which he began the third week. He spoke at length and vigorously, inviting questions and queries on specific lines.

First he describes the nature of Elizabethan theatre, which would have been performed in the open air, to one to two thousand people of all classes. Verse, with its useful rhetorical devices, was the obvious way to reach them. Besides, with a heritage of medieval mystery plays, and the verse of Chaucer, they would have been familiar with alliteration, antithesis and apposition and would have understood the emotional import of monosyllabic lines and had a relish for the language generally.

'By the time he wrote *Antony and Cleopatra*,' Hall continues, 'Shakespeare had more mastery of the verse than ever before (Harley Granville Barker's "exploiting freedom to the full, he has forged an instrument of extraordinary suppleness and resource"). He also had a company of actors who had grown up with its devices and rhythms, through the very regular scansion and plentiful rhymes of his early plays, to the freer form of the later ones. Keeping to the beat of the line makes it fleet: Hamlet's instruction to the Players, that the speech be spoken "trippingly on the tongue", is worth all of Stanislavski in doing Shakespeare.' 'Hamlet was addressing a band of actors who had slogged in Shakespearean rep; the rhythm had got into their heads.'

He continues: 'Since we don't have the same opportunities now, the modern temptation is to think "since it doesn't scan in an obvious way, let's not bother to scan at all". Wrong! And I'm unashamedly pedantic about this: it may need a beat, an elision, but every single line in Shakespeare will scan. Your business is to find and keep as close to the five beats of the iambic pentameter as possible and then decide on what's right for you in terms of emphasis and colour. I suggest you find the two words that need bringing out:

> Nay, but this dótage of our general's
> O'erflows the méasure.

It's exactly comparable to music (think of Mozart's *The Marriage of Figaro*): once you have the phrasing right you can manoeuvre within it. By modernizing, not keeping to the beat, we hold the verse up, make it slower, and the play loses its tension – and its hold on our attention.'

Some history followed: Hall described how only he, John Barton and Trevor Nunn could pass on this rediscovered way of handling Shakespearean verse, having been trained in it by George Rylands at Cambridge, and then able to implement it in their direction at the RSC. Rylands had received it from William Poël, the famous Elizabethan specialist, an enormous influence on the staging of Shakespeare in the early part of the century. Peter Hall had learned a lot, too, from Edith Evans, herself a protégé of Poël's. (Edith Evans: 'Shakespeare has this wonderful rhythm which my old master taught me. You learn to go from emphatic word to emphatic word like a springboard, and then, if you want to slow up, you lean on them a bit.') This is something the actors in *Antony and Cleopatra* are discovering: that both the sense of a line and its emotional content are clearly indicated once they find the pulse of the metre. It can release tremendous energy in them.

Next, the linear structure. 'The weight runs on to the end of the line where the verb usually is. At the end of a line without a full stop, you get the expectancy of what is coming at the caesura in the next line, so make towards that. Breathe where there is a full stop – at the end of the line, or in the caesura breaks; sometimes you'll have to take an imperceptible breath in between.' (The scripts being used by the cast, taken from the First Folio, have the early punctuation and not that amended – and sometimes falsified – by some later scholar.)

'You must find your own way of marking the end of each line. It's not a hold-up but a release of energy: Peggy Ashcroft uses emphasis, John Gielgud sings it. It's idiosyncratic. All these things are clues to actors, but Shakespeare is absolutely flexible. He doesn't imprison himself or you.

'Obviously, where there's a half-line and another character takes over, it's a cue to complete within the metre and you need a good "feed" from your fellow actor, as with comedy. It's just like baroque music: in Monteverdi, at the same moment you come to the end of one line, the melody begins on the next. . . .'

'Monosyllabic lines need to be splayed out, are heavier, more emotional. They are not rhetoric but indicate a need to point up some significance. It's up to you to fill them as you like, following the usual iambic pentameter length. If you beat a monosyllabic line in a regular way, you'll be too quick:

> I have myself resolved upon a course   (10 beats)
> Which has no need of you.   Be gone.   (8 beats)

'Rhymes are to be relished, not avoided. They are comic or romantic in his comedies. Shakespeare often finished a scene with a rhyming couplet. There's not a lot of rhyme in *Antony and Cleopatra*. He had begun to fall out of love with it.

'There's a lot of apposition (balance) and antithesis:

> As is the morn-dew on the myrtle leaf
> To his grand sea

as well as alliteration and assonance. The English of Shakespeare's time was extremely resonant, the vowels rich, somewhere between a Belfast accent and that of a Pennsylvanian mountain community, both of which were settled by English Protestants in the seventeenth century. As they were cut off, the accent remained largely unchanged. We can do nothing about these lost sounds, but can give the words their colour.' (Peter Hall reads the opening lines of the play in Elizabethan English and gets a round of delighted applause: it is an organic and satisfying sound.)

'Verse and prose are often interspersed. Although Shakespeare probably didn't do it consciously, emotional pressure leads to prose breaking into verse, self-control returns verse to prose. Verse is quicker, fleeter, prose more angular, laid out, used for the ironic, cynical speeches, or to indicate rage.

'I'd like us to relish and colour the words as much as possible. It's not fashionable, but it's appropriate for this play. All these characters know they're on a world stage. The language has to be felt and lived and invented as you speak it. In *Antony and Cleopatra* where it is so physical, so vibrant, we should endorse it . . . although it may become like clotted cream. Despite a groundswell of subtext, this is extrovert writing which says what it feels.'

He pauses, sympathetically, for Judi Dench's response – 'Yes, but the difficulty is making it accessible. The play is to do with all the things we know about, but the emotion does come so much on the line' – then continues.

'Most of Shakespeare's phrasing is not as we or even his colleagues would have done it. Find out what he's saying and how: key words must be reconciled with the beat. If it doesn't scan without eliding words, then that's the indication to run them together.' Hall repeats a favourite jazz analogy: 'Find the beat, the ongoing rhythm; then you can do anything.'

In conclusion, he stresses that he would rather hear mis-scanned Shakespeare that's alive, than scanned Shakespeare that's dead – but he would prefer the best of both. . . . 'I beg you, don't see this as a frightful imprisonment: it's the very opposite, it frees you, and the new discipline will add to your strength.'

Whilst Hall has been speaking, there has been an alertness, a tension in the actors' listening: these are challenging insights, tools, they are about to have the chance to apply. The rehearsal that follows has a heightened awareness, not just for the participants, but for an observer like myself.

Through years of grounding with Peter Hall and the RSC, Judi Dench is finely attuned to the language and all its clues: each full stop indicates a new thought; the emotion is impacted and simultaneous to each phrase. Her handling of the scansion by now innate ('You work at it, work at it and suddenly it becomes a part of you which you never lose'), she has the freedom and confidence to experiment, using the verse as a springboard.

Anthony Hopkins has been saying that he found this a much richer play than *Lear*, a response, perhaps, not so much to the content of either, but to Hall's approach to the verse. Quite new to him, he finds it immensely exciting and enabling; there is an almost physical relish of the language, a pleasure in mastering its shape and colouring.

With a body of Shakespearean work behind him (including two previous productions of *Antony and Cleopatra* with the RSC), Tim Pigott-Smith has an accomplished delivery and style. Yet, from the time rehearsals on this production started, he has been absorbing Hall's guidance on the verse with the fervour of a novitiate: 'The language is marvellous. By following the scansion, you find the sense and the emotion works for itself. You don't have to pump it out.'

Pigott-Smith says that it was Simon Callow's experience working with Hall on the sonnets that made him want to be in this production. Iain Ormsby-Knox (playing Mardian), says that Hall's talk is 'emblazoned across his heart'.

I express surprise to Hall himself that this, his approach to Shakespeare, is such a revelation to actors who are otherwise very experienced. At Stratford he had first taught Judi Dench and other actors such as Ian Holm, Vanessa Redgrave, David Warner, Ian Richardson, Alan Howard and Janet Suzman. This was, moreover, within a framework in which the skills involved could be continually reinforced. Now, however, since most directors avoid confronting the structure of the verse at all, actors doing Shakespeare are left to flounder – and Hall is well aware that he will have to teach for most if not all of the rehearsal period of *Antony and Cleopatra*.

Actors used to approaching their lines via psychological motivation find it very difficult to work through the rhythm of the text to a sense of these lines. Voice coach Julia Wilson-Dixon provides me with an overview: earlier in the century Shakespearean acting became trapped in a rigid adherence to form. Naturalistic acting, when the verse flattened into prose, was a healthy and inevitable reaction: 'They ignored the ends of lines, ran on to the middle of the next. But how much freedom does anarchy give? One must work towards a synthesis which marries form with sense and emotion. *That* is liberating: and it is what Peter Hall took from George Rylands (who had revived the Poël/Granville Barker tradition) and put into practice with the RSC.'

How relevant becomes the credo of Harley Granville Barker, expressed almost sixty years ago in the Introduction to his Prefaces:

> When it comes to staging the plays, the speaking of the
> verse must be the foundation of all study. . . . If we are
> to make Shakespeare our own again we must be put to a
> little trouble about it. We must recapture as far as may
> be his lost meanings; and the sense of a phrase we *can*
> recapture, though instinctive emotional response to it
> may be a loss for ever. The tunes that he writes to, the
> whole art of his great music-making, we can master.
> Actors can train their ears and tongues and can train our
> ears to it. We talk of lost arts. No art is ever lost while
> the means to it survive. Our faculties rust by disuse and
> by misuse are coarsened, but they quickly recover
> delight in a beautiful thing.

Perhaps therein lies an antidote to Hall's 'we are probably living in the last fifty years in which this language is communicable'?

Following his talk, Peter Hall is even more exacting about the language: he constantly draws attention to pauses, instances of alliteration ('profit . . . prayers', 'field of feasts'), apposition ('It makes for immediate clarity when you embrace them – "gods . . . men", "Rome . . . Egypt"'), pulling out key words for emphasis, correcting an actor who keeps saying 'in' for 'by'. Meaning is clarified: '"Mark Antony . . . will make/ No wars without doors" – but he's making lots of wars within, in his love combats with Cleopatra.' The director is also encouraging: praising David Schofield's 'wonderful ability to speak on the tongue', he urges him to make use of it to express Pompey's caprices.

'All the soliloquies are directed out front,' says Hall. 'Can you believe otherwise? Elizabethan actors were facing an audience of one to two thousand. The introspection of Hamlet is a nineteenth-century convention. He'd have been asking an audience for advice: "Shall I be or not be . . .?"

'The danger with asides is to make them confidential: they are a public and truthful address to the audience.'

Archetypes are defined in musical terms. Antony is Mars, basso: 'Da-dum-pa-pom. It's C Major,' intones Hall. Caesar is minor-keyed and sharp: 'Neh-neh-neh-niggle-niggle,' obliges Tim Pigott-Smith. Demonstrating a line, the director puts in an extra 'the' which Michael Bryant jumps on. Pigott-Smith: 'Now you know how we feel.' Peter Hall: 'I *know* how you feel. That's why I do what I do and not what you do!'

Working on a scene (Act III Scene 4) between Antony and Octavia, Hall, as ever, digs into the text for its clues: 'The problem is how to come on in the middle of a row. Shakespeare does this to us often. . . . Tony, you'll manage it rhythmically if you take a breath:

> . . . that and the thousands more (*breath*)
> Of semblable import, but he hath waged (*big breath*)
> New wars 'gainst Pompey, made his will and read it (*breath*)
> (*hit 'read'*)
> To public ear, (*long pause – for it's this that offends him*)

'Methinks Antony doth protest too much. In his next speech every full stop indicates a change of thought: he's looking for a way out.

'Sally, look at the pauses in Octavia's speech: she waits but he doesn't respond. At a half-line, you've got to build up, give the appropriate "feed":

OCTAVIA   . . . . no midway
            'Twixt these extremes at all. (*Hand it to him*)
ANTONY   Gentle Octavia, . . .

'Her emotion almost breaks through in the repetition of "most weak, most weak". Then:

> Wars 'twixt you twain would be   (*big breath*)
> As if the world should cleave and that slain men
>   (*hyperbole – you carry the audience along with you*)
> Should solder up the rift.

'Since Antony's attempt to "go straight" hasn't worked at all, he resents her deeply. Listen to the steely coldness in:

Peter Hall directs *Antony and Cleopatra*
— Rehearsal Room 1

Judi Dench — Cleopatra

Anthony Hopkins — Mark Antony   Tim Pigott-Smith — Octavius Caesar

The Roman Triumvirate
Tim Pigott-Smith, John Bluthal (Lepidus),
Anthony Hopkins.   *Act II Scene 2*

Discussing the 'Summit Conference'.   *Act II Scene 2*

Alison Chitty's early costume designs.
Top left: Antony; top right: Cleopatra;
left: Soothsayer; right: Mardian's Bull's Head mask

Basil Henson (Agrippa), Graham Sinclair (Maecenas), Michael Bryant (Enobarbus)
ENOBARBUS: The barge she sat in . . . Burned on the water. *Act II Scene 2*

Sally Dexter (Octavia), Peter Hall, Anthony Hopkins
ANTONY: . . . that to come./Shall all be done by th' rule. *Act II Scene 3*

David Schofield (Pompey); Peter Gordon (Menecrates)
and Michael Carter (Menas) at rear.
POMPEY: I shall do well./The people love me and the sea is mine.
Act II Scene 1

From designer Alison Chitty's sketchbook — Pompey's galley,
'an image from da Vinci's *Last Supper*'.   *Act II Scene 7*

POMPEYS GALLEY

HAMMOCKS : + BEAMS :

POMPEYS GALLEY - UNDER OARS.

ROPES + SAILS,
+ BUMBERS."

Judi Dench and Anthony Hopkins

ANTONY: Our separation so abides and flies
That thou residing here goes yet with me,
And our hence fleeting here remain with thee.

Act I Scene 3

*Ch*oose your own *c*ompany and *c*ommand what *c*ost. . . .'

The actors struggle to reconcile the technical with the intellectual and emotional, to retain the necessary degree of objectivity whilst tapping internal resources.

As rehearsals progress, Hall's argument is to become manifest: Hopkins' characteristic staccato is interspersed with waves of lyricism, Tim Pigott-Smith is incisive, his phrasing informed by Caesar's calculated intelligence, John Bluthal's Lepidus overflows with pacifying mellifluence, Basil Henson is measured caution, his stresses subtly making their point, Bryant so modulates the verse as to give it the hesitations of improvised speech. Although they all hold to the iambic pentameter, there is still scope for the widest individuality.

Late January sunshine: in the rehearsal room, a strip of blue sky can be seen through the dormer windows and there are vases of daffodils on the stage management tables.

After Hall's talk on the language, they spend the third week of rehearsal going 'from the top again', working through the play scene by scene with fresh insights.

As the actors have begun to memorize their words, there is much more physical interaction between them. The opening procession of the Egyptian court evolves: Cleopatra drags Mardian in on the end of a rope, with Antony sitting on his shoulders, waving a wine-flagon and goblet. Charmian and Iras weave round them and flirt with Alexas. Once Antony dismounts, the lovers prowl round one another, she teasing, he lunging at her. 'It's like a gnat buzzing round a bull', is Judi Dench's image.

For the first time, Tony Hopkins seems to have shed the shadow of *Lear*. He comes across as robust and youthful, an heroic, winning character who loves and knows he is loved.

Towards the end of the week, John Haynes comes in to take rehearsal photographs of *Antony and Cleopatra*. (An exhibition of his work, then on in the National's foyer, showed legendary productions of the last twenty years.) A slight figure, dressed in black, Haynes moves in on the 'summit conference' to capture Caesar and Antony shaking hands across a smiling Lepidus, throwing the highly public nature of the play into surreal perspective. These are media figures depicted at key moments in history. Today, their every move would be covered by newsreel footage. Antony's defection to Egypt and the affair between him and Cleopatra would attract the paparazzi, produce scandalous headlines. . . .

CHAPTER 4

The 'Meat' of the Piece

WEEK 5 – Monday 9 February

The actors were given the fourth week off, to polish up on their lines. When they reassemble, the company moves into what had been called the 'meat' of the piece: having blocked in the canvas with their first responses, they are ready to get to grips with emotional and intellectual detail, to probe under the skin to blood, sinew and gristle.

We are now into the 'three days and nights of battle', begun when Antony and Cleopatra declared their intention of fighting by sea at Actium. In Act III Scene 11, they were, literally, grounded by defeat, sitting in despair and isolation on opposite sides of the stage.

In Act III Scene 12 they send a Schoolmaster to Caesar to sue for peace on their behalf. Tim Pigott-Smith (surrounded by Agrippa, Dolabella, Thidias and others): 'He's never performed this function before and we really nail him. Let's make it very public and embarrassing, by spilling the court around him. Come on, man, advance!'

Peter Hall: 'And he botches it, out of nerves'. Peter Gordon, bespectacled, plays it overwhelmed with humility, stuttering out Antony's request to live in Egypt or, a private man, in Athens. Cleopatra, acknowledging Caesar's supremacy, begs 'The circle of the Ptolemies for her heirs'. Caesar responds harshly: if Cleopatra drives Antony from Egypt (or kills him), she 'shall not sue unheard'. Peter Hall: 'It's like talking to granite.' The contrasts make the scene surprisingly poignant: the reversal of power is painfully under-lined. (Basil Henson, Agrippa, escorts the Schoolmaster out – and leads him the wrong way. Alan Cohen: 'He's taking him for a consoling drink!')

Andrew Wadsworth (Dolabella) is in Caesar's entourage. Because both Dolabella and Scarus (Wadsworth's other role) enter late in the play, the actor has hardly been at rehearsals until now, and needs reassurance about what he is doing. He and Hall (who have worked together on *Martine* and *Coming into Land*) share an ongoing joke about 'leaving ego and paranoia at the Stage Door' and exchanging them for 'Industry, Imagination and Intelligence' – the three I's of Ellen Terry. In fact, Wadsworth (despite having played leads in such West End musicals as *Sweeney Todd*, *Oklahoma* and *Guys and Dolls*) is nervous. Why is it always a surprise to discover that extremely experienced actors can be, too?

Act III Scene 13. Antony is enraged and humiliated by Caesar's answer: 'To the boy Caesar send this grizzled head' he tells Cleopatra, and he'll grant your wishes. (For this Hopkins uses a grotesquely effective gesture – yanking his own head up by the hair as if it were already severed). Ludicrously, Antony dares Caesar to fight him in single combat, for the fate of the Roman Empire. Re-entering, he finds Caesar's ambassador, Thidias (Des Adams), kissing Cleopatra's hand. Hopkins: 'Can I leave him in some doubt about what I'm going to do to him?' So he starts off quietly, almost courteously, then suddenly erupts, in a relish of rage and violence. He is like a wounded lion, pumping out fury, summoning servants to drag Thidias away and whip him. The howling and bellowing is oppressive and, at times, almost unintelligible. Some actors put the brakes on when first dealing with big emotional scenes, distancing themselves: Tony Hopkins' characteristic head-on approach takes courage (under the judging eyes of other actors). It is also hellish difficult, within the arrested flow of stop/start rehearsing, to tap all this emotion whilst still grappling with the words.

Peter Hall waits on the sidelines, then moves in to modulate, using the energy but showing Hopkins how to control it: 'You are now in command of the breathing, the scansion and the rhythm. Choose your way through the lines. It breaks down, Tony, into the big, over-the-top curses, and the cruel, low-voiced threats. It needs to have light and shade. Change the tone at every full stop. Come at each new thought differently.'

Cleopatra manages to assure Antony of her continuing devotion and he quietens. (Hall underlines the desperation of their situation: Antony has lost most of his troops and things seem hopeless. Yet she tries to comfort him and give him backbone. She has grown up a bit

after Actium, learned to hold her tongue and be supportive.) Enobarbus' decision to leave Antony provides a dark commentary on
the foreground action.

Act IV Scene 1. Caesar ridicules the actions of 'the old ruffian'. He
is fully in command of himself, in pointed contrast to Antony as we
have just seen him. They try this scene (Caesar reading Antony's
letter of challenge) with Pigott-Smith standing on a table (as if in one
of the balconies overlooking the Olivier stage). It does not work.
When he repeats it down amongst his soldiers and generals, content
and action gell.

Act IV Scene 2. Antony, further humiliated by Caesar's refusal to
fight him singly, calls in his household servants to say goodbye. Peter
Hall has talked about the tragedy of a great man fallen, almost out of
his mind. 'This is usually done as a touching scene; in fact, it's
maudlin and disgusting. Antony's enormous self-pity frightens those
round him:

> May be it is the period of your duty.
> Haply you shall not see me more, or if,
> A mangled shadow.

The democratic stuff is very suspect:

> . . . make as much of me
> As when my empire was your fellow too
> And suffered my command.

If a leader tries to put across "I'm just like you", the reaction is "So
why is he in charge?"'

Cleopatra and her entourage form a dismayed semi-circle upstage.
This display of Antony's – whom he accuses of making them all
'onion-eyed' – will prove to be the last straw for Enobarbus. The
servants creep on from behind the screen stage left, John Bluthal
very funny as a simple, overwhelmed menial. Finally Antony says:

> Let's to supper, come
> And drown consideration.

It is a half-line to which no one responds: the irony is that Antony is
already needing to be propped up.

Act IV Scene 3. Soldiers on nightwatch hear 'Music i'th'air' and
'Under the earth':

IST SOLDIER   What should this mean?
2ND SOLDIER   'Tis the great god Hercules whom Antony
loved,
Now leaves him. . . .

This is a deeply perturbing symbol of the latter's ebbing powers.

As always, Peter Hall has paced the scene through in the blocking, spent time considering its choreography. He invites further suggestions from the four actors involved. Should they move through the auditorium? Use the balconies on either side of the Olivier stage? Bring on more soldiers?

Act IV Scene 4. Too restless to sleep, Antony is having his armour buckled on by Eros, before going back into battle. It is a wonderful morning. He feels rejuvenated. Cleopatra feels twenty-five again. She is kittenish, tries playfully to help.

Hall: 'The audience will run the undercurrent of unease for you from the previous scenes; you can just play it up front. There is a sense in which she and Antony see themselves as great actors upon the world of the stage. When there isn't anything happening, the adrenalin doesn't flow. They need to be "the great lovers", "the tragic hero", "the paramour", using extravagant gestures which are also slightly tacky.'

When Antony goes off with his soldiers, Cleopatra momentarily reveals her misgivings, giving a sting to the tail of the scene.

Act IV Scene 5. Another 'en passant' scene, which had been blocked so as to give it the clamour of preparation for battle. Carrying his helmet, a Soldier runs across the stage encountering Antony who, optimism renewed, is on his way to fight. Recognizing the man as the same who had warned him not to fight by sea at Actium, Antony says openly:

Would thou and those thy scars had once prevailed
To make me fight by land!

When the Soldier inadvertently discloses that Enobarbus, Antony's companion-at-arms, has left him, it is a shattering blow. Although Eros tries to comfort his master ('but his luggage is still here . . .'), Antony is not to be placated; he blames himself:

O my fortunes have corrupted honest men!

Act IV Scene 6. Caesar, confident of success, predicts a 'time of universal peace'. Enobarbus, defected to Caesar's camp, is brought news that Antony has sent all his treasure after him, and added more. ('Your emperor/Continues still a Jove', says the Soldier, young Welsh actor Paddy Brennan, whom I had watched the day before, working on the vocal mechanics of these same lines, with Julia Wilson-Dixon.) Overwhelmed by remorse, Enobarbus resolves to seek 'Some ditch wherein to die'.

Act IV Scene 7. The course of the second battle is sketched in, with Agrippa leading Caesar's soldiers across the stage, Antony and his men in hot pursuit. How to deploy the actors available? Will they disappear with Agrippa, only to reappear in Antony's train, under different banners? (Since this is a civil war, battledress does not change.) This is a scene of totally unexpected victory for Antony: Caesar's troops are forced to retreat.

Act IV Scene 8. Antony cannot believe he has won. Confidence in his prowess restored, he is his former generous, warm self again. For the triumphal return to Alexandria, he and his soldiers, accompanied by drum rolls, will come down the centre aisle of the theatre and up on to the stage, with the doors rolling back before them. Hall: 'Don't get too military.' Charmian and Iras wait in the doorway as Cleopatra emerges, to be greeted by full bows of Elizabethan gallantry.

Peter Hall wants 'a sense of the miraculous' and urges space between her and Antony. The lyrical language is enormously moving as they face one another, first apart in wonderment, then moving in to embrace, after Antony's exultant

> O thou day o'th'world
> Chain mine armed neck, leap thou, attire and all,
> Through proofs of harness to my heart and there
> Ride on the pants triumphing.

Act IV Scene 9. Enobarbus dies of a broken heart – and Michael Bryant has to find the extremity of emotion whilst hanging on to the character's credibility: 'It's difficult not to get carried away. . . .' Hall only intervenes to suggest that he drop to his knees halfway through his final speech, so as to crumple to the ground by degrees.

Act IV Scene 10. Tony Hopkins and Andrew Wadsworth (Scarus) face out front: Antony has given orders for his troops to engage with Caesar's upon the sea. Although he is full of bravado and still seems obsessed about winning in every element (even 'i'th'fire or i'th'air'), it is significant that he has not put out to sea himself; it is an element which now terrifies him, emblematic of his failure at Actium and of his ruinous enthralment to Cleopatra – whom he once called Thetis, the sea nymph.

Act IV Scene 12. Scarus speaks of Antony's confusion of emotions: hope and fear. Recorded sound effects of battle will end with a great cheer for Caesar – Antony's fleet have yielded to the enemy. Antony is at once convinced that Cleopatra has betrayed him ('Triple-turned whore! . . . my heart/Makes only wars on thee'). All is over: 'this pine is barked/That overtopped them all'. She, for whom he sacrificed everything, has 'Beguiled me to the very heart of loss'.

Here the play becomes intensely moving, almost unbearably tragic. The clue has to be the middle-agedness of them both, the sense that all *is* truly over, they will not have the chance to make a comeback. I had always before seen the relationship played as youthfully as possible, as that of a couple in their prime. But these are two with their best behind them, their greatness now in tatters.

When Cleopatra appears, Antony turns on her in maddened rage as if he would tear her to pieces. The three days and nights of battle are at an end.

In Act IV Scene 13 Charmian persuades Cleopatra to lock herself in the monument and send word to Antony that she is dead.

Tony Hopkins has become increasingly depressed about learning his lines, trying to struggle through rehearsals with prompting, sometimes giving up and returning to his script. (At one point Judi Dench takes his hands in sympathy: 'It's agony, isn't it? Getting through that great wad of words that first time without the book. . . .') Hall persuades him to take a few days off until he feels confident about the lines: the cast respond with quick understanding.

(Blaming himself for the problem, Hopkins might well have derived comfort from some remarks I only came across once the production had opened: 'I had great difficulty, for the first time, in learning the lines, partly because it's chopped up, short sentences, short phrases' – Michael Redgrave on his own portrayal of Antony in 1953.)

Act IV Scene 14. When they get to this scene, in which Eros kills himself, followed by Antony's falling on his sword, Hall concentrates on its emotional complexity: Eros' devotion to his master, the Roman concept of honourable suicide, Antony's deep shame that Cleopatra (or so he believes) and Eros have had the courage to die by their own hand before him.

Antony is fatally wounded but not dead:

> I have done my work ill friends. O make an end
> Of what I have begun.

No one has the courage or the heart to do so. Then Antony hears that Cleopatra is still alive and the scene ends as he is borne away to the monument, stoic and magnanimous at the last:

>   Bid that welcome
> Which comes to punish us, and we punish it
> Seeming to bear it lightly. Take me up.
> I have led you oft; carry me now, good friends,
> And have my thanks for all.

Act IV Scene 15. The monument is set up: Judi Dench cautiously climbs the staircase on wheels, clutching the rail.

During blocking, they had talked about the logistics and general shape of this scene up to Antony's death. Now they go into more detail, breaking it up: Cleopatra is in a strangely pessimistic mood which her women have never seen before. Her language gives hints of impending death and the majesty to which she will rise. When Antony is carried in, her first instinct is self-preservation; not for anything will she risk coming down to him. (Dench: 'And later, when he asks for wine and wants to talk, she says "Oh no, let *me* speak".') 'Why does she mention Octavia now?' asks Hall. Dench: 'She's obsessed by her. Octavia is "the other woman".'

After Antony is hauled up we get a refrain of their relationship as it used to be – the joy, the wine, the love, their supremacy. Twice, in his death throes, Antony says, 'I am dying, Egypt, dying'. Hall points out that, in modern terms, one 'dies of love'; in camp Elizabethan jargon, to die was to have an orgasm. This scene, then, is also the final consummation of their passion.

Then he dies and she seems to go into a trance. Hall coaches Miranda Foster and Helen Fitzgerald in the irregular scansion of:

IRAS   She's dead too, our sovereign
CHARMIAN   Lady!
IRAS   Madam!

He works with great delicacy, probing for the clues in the language: 'O madam, madam, madam/Royal Egypt!/Empress!/Peace, peace, Iras!' has a rhythmic, oriental keening tone. Cleopatra, waking from her trance, rejects its emotionalism in resolving that they die stoically, 'after the high Roman fashion'. Now she is much more realistic, hollow of all emotion. Life having lost its meaning with Antony's death ('Our lamp is spent') her mind is racing towards 'the briefest end'.

There is nothing sentimental or neurotic about Judi Dench: all of a piece, her approach to the large emotions is non-reverential, almost domestic. (Why do I remember her automatically gathering up everyone's dishes after lunch in the canteen?) Access to even the darkest moments in the play is controlled by brisk wit, a burrowing intelligence and a practical reactive streak.

Hall had talked about the shift of tension in the final section of the play, after Antony's death. Cleopatra is now pitted against Caesar; her means of rejoining Antony is a last wave to be crested. . . . (The monument is rolled back.)

Act V Scene 1. Hall: 'I'd like to wipe the stage with energy after that still monument scene.' Caesar is in a strange, high-keyed mood. Tim Pigott-Smith wonders whether 'the very odd scansion' he has found reflects emotional pressure. To Michael Carter (as Decretas, bearing Antony's bloodied sword) Hall urges a rolling declamation of the momentous news of Antony's death. He instructs Michael Bottle (the 'poor Egyptian' sent from Cleopatra to know Caesar's intentions) to be as obsequious as possible: 'She's picked her man carefully.' 'Ah, a Dickensian Egyptian!' responds the actor.

Many pauses are indicated as Caesar works out his tactics: he will send Proculeius (Brian Spink, in his third Roman incarnation) to soften Cleopatra up and prevent her killing herself, before storming the monument. In order to externalize Caesar's accelerated thinking, Pigott-Smith suggests that the pauses be filled by Proculeius crossing, to be stopped by another idea of Caesar's, moving, halted by a further thought: 'And . . . and . . . and . . . gets me heated up.'

Caesar's main feeling is guilt for the downfall of two mythological figures. Introducing *Antony and Cleopatra*, Hall had spoken of each character's concern to be interpreted well, both in their time and by posterity. Now Caesar must prove his probity and gentleness: he urges Agrippa and Maecenas to see 'in all my writings' how he was drawn into this war against his will.

Clearly, honour has little to do with its practice but is very bound up with public image. It almost seems to depend on a figurative 'having the last word' – which preoccupies Antony at the approach of his death:

> Not Caesar's valour hath o'erthrown Antony
> But Antony's hath triumphed on itself . . .

and which will lead Cleopatra to pursue her own, to cheat Caesar of holding her up to public ridicule in Rome, where:

> The quick comedians
> Extemporally will stage us. . . . Antony
> Shall be brought drunken forth and I shall see
> Some squeaking Cleopatra boy my greatness
> I'th'posture of a whore.

Act V Scene 2 returns us to the monument:

PROCULEIUS (*beat*)   My name is Proculeius. (*beat*)
CLEOPATRA   Antony
(*long pause – the naming recalls him*)
Did tell me of you, bade me trust you. . . .

She is halfway to death yet Proculeius' presence seduces her back to life and the cat-and-mouse game of politics. She slips in that she would like to see Caesar although (wryly) 'I am his fortune's vassal', a nobody: her purpose – to ensure her son Caesarion's future.

Once captured, she tries to stab herself. Disarmed, she goes berserk. (Hall: 'Tries to run on to a soldier's sword?') Dench: 'It's more like a terrible cry than a running-about thing. Throwing her down from the monument is an awful abusing.' At first, the actress builds to a high note at the end ('Say I would die'). Then re-runs the speech:

> Sir, I will eat no meat, I'll not drink, sir;
>   . . . This mortal house I'll ruin,

starting with violence and dropping to a low intensity.

Dolabella is sent to pacify her. He comes in very cocky and is then stricken by her rhapsodizing: 'I dreamt there was an emperor Antony . . .' (which Dench does almost literally, in a dream, absolutely still; foiled and humiliated, Cleopatra has turned in on herself). Dolabella, moved by her grief, reveals Caesar's plans to lead her in triumph to Rome.

The entry of Caesar himself is full of brittleness: beneath the diplomatic language, a chilling bargaining goes on. In him Cleopatra quickly recognizes that she has met her match: he alone is impervious to her charms, not to be wooed. One feels the cold wind of a new, pragmatic era, that of Augustus Caesar, in which romantic passion, and its excess, will play no part. The revelation by her treasurer Seleucus, that Cleopatra has concealed the true value of her possessions, is another betrayal.

Dench finds the emotional switches difficult ('They're so fluctuating, so knife-edge. . .'). 'She's desperate to keep negotiations going to vouchsafe her children,' offers Hall.

In fact, by the time of Caesar's exit, Cleopatra knows that she can expect nothing from him. After despatching Charmian for the snakes, she prepares Iras by painting a mordantly humorous picture, a Grimm's fairy tale, almost, of what life holds. The queen is 'again for Cydnus/To meet Mark Antony'.

Taking the basket of figs (and asps) from the Clown, in a gently humorous exchange, she has her last contact with the outside world. (John Bluthal, intrigued by the multiple ways of playing the scene, produces a book of Shakespearean criticism which dwells on its Freudian connotations.)

Finally, tended by her women, royally attired, Cleopatra rises to death with a kind of ecstasy:

> I am fire and air, my other elements
> I give to baser life.

Some of her lines have a delicate wit, there is glee in calling Caesar 'ass unpolicied', whilst she waits for the poison to take effect. She dies serenely, mid-sentence.

Iras having already expired on Cleopatra's farewell kiss, devoted Charmian alone remains to straighten her mistress' crown and seal her eyes. She holds the asp to herself as the Guard raises the alarm.

Caesar and all his train break in upon the dreamlike intimacy of the

previous scene. Cause of death having been ascertained, the new
Roman emperor gives instructions for Cleopatra's burial:

> She shall be buried by her Antony;
> No grave upon the earth shall clip in it
> A pair so famous.
>   . . . Our army shall
> In solemn show attend this funeral
> And then to Rome.

The play ends with sombre ceremonial as the bodies are borne away.

The play is still difficult to encompass but sections are beginning to
have texture and shape. It is like complicated architecture. Increasingly, an understanding of how to move through the building –
its articulation – will emerge.

CHAPTER 5

Publicity and Programme: Historical Research

'In the theatre, two things matter most,' says John Goodwin, Head of Publicity and Publications at the National. 'What you put on the stage – and getting people to come and see it.'

A colleague of Hall's for almost thirty years, both at the RSC and on the South Bank, Goodwin edited his *Diaries*, working from tape transcripts over three years.

As head of a team of NT publicists deployed on individual productions, his priority is his work with the media. The coverage thus generated is the most effective means of spreading the word about what the theatre has to offer. He also controls advertising and every piece of print – programme, poster, press release and repertoire leaflet – that the NT puts out, the envoy to the public of its policies and plans.

Some shows need more selling than others and his budget for publicity is juggled accordingly (it is £107,000 for 1986/87, about £60,000 of which will be recouped in profits from programmes and other publications). Advertising, handled via an agency, is the major expenditure.

John Goodwin manages to be always courteous whilst working to constant deadlines – an in-house document about the current position in a union negotiation, material about the National Theatre for an American journalist, a programme lay-out which has to be passed. With fifteen or sixteen new productions a year, pressure depends on the intervals between their opening dates. Unlike the RSC and the opera houses, where forthcoming plans cover a season and can be announced intact before each, the NT runs continuously. Press conferences are therefore flexible, held either to meet a crisis (and the NT has had many of different kinds) or to pass on those of the coming year's plans which are known with any certainty.

Specific information about *Antony and Cleopatra* – the cast, production team and opening dates – was circulated, once confirmed, to seven hundred media outlets. From then on, Nicki Frei, the particular publicist working on it, has been following up with personal letters and telephone calls to journalists, suggesting ideas for media coverage. Photo sessions and interviews (press, radio and television) are arranged well in advance, especially with magazines and Sunday colour supplements in which space is allocated months ahead. Frei's publicizing network extends beyond Britain to Europe and America, reaching the potential tourist market.

The need to plant the play very firmly in the eye of the public must be balanced with any reservations the actors may have: Tony Hopkins feels he has had overmuch publicity exposure in the past two years. As rehearsals for *Antony and Cleopatra* progress and the onus for its critical reception begins to weigh heavily on them, both he and Judi Dench worry that the steady stream of interviews and photo-calls could 'overhype' the play before it opens.

Because this is a National Theatre production with a prestigious 'package' – of classical play, high-profile director and actors – media interest is assured. Nevertheless, a high degree of sensitivity and skill is needed to position the production appropriately and to time the flow of publicity so that it gradually builds up towards the opening, with enough momentum to keep interest (and seat sales) going through the run.

John Goodwin has talked about the need to create audiences for the future, to reach schoolchildren. Did that mean that he believed in the theatre's potential for mass appeal?

'It is and must be our ambition to attract a public beyond the core theatre-going audience, but theatre is a minority interest and always will be – and in a sense that is its strength,' is his conviction. 'For if that changed, it would change the whole character of theatre – affecting the plays you put on, the nature of the writing and presentation – very possibly, weakening it. One source of the power of theatre is that it has an audience which is, on the whole, worldly – so you can be confident about breaking established convention in what you say and do onstage. Theatre is a very free form, without the financial pressures of film-making, or the cautions imposed upon television because it is seen by millions in their own homes. A yardstick of how much theatre matters, its extraordinary influence, is the enormous exposure it gets in the media in proportion to the comparatively small number of people who see it.'

From a man who has championed the theatre for forty years, this is a mature view I have to respect, although I baulk at it. Why shouldn't really thrilling, powerful theatre, operating on levels beyond the intellectual, hook a popular audience? That this does not happen is not an absolute, but a reflection of our particular era and socio-political framework, the kind of theatre we offer and the elitist aura it has assumed. It is certainly a reflection of our educational divide. The Greek amphitheatre pulled in audiences of fifteen thousand, the Elizabethan open-air theatre, one to two thousand . . . isn't it too simple to attribute the diminution of numbers to the rival attractions of television and film alone? Ibsen said that the absolutely imperative task of democracy was to make aristocrats of us all: aristocrats of expectation and response to the theatre, too?

That said, and as John Goodwin later pointed out, over 100,000 people were to have seen *Antony and Cleopatra* by the time its run ended – for a minority interest, that's not *un*popular.

A first meeting to discuss the programme and poster is presided over by Goodwin, and attended by the print manager Lynn Haill, Michael Mayhew (in charge of graphic design), Richard Bird (who designs most of the NT posters), his assistant Rose Towler, and Nicki Frei. Such is his reliance on John Goodwin, Hall does not attend, but he and Alison Chitty have suggested Veronese's *Mars and Venus Bound by Cupid* for the poster and programme cover. Permission to reproduce it, and a slide of the original, will be got from the Metropolitan Museum in New York; (it is finally reproduced in sepia mezzotint, with orange and white lettering, handsomely establishing the Renaissance spirit of the production).

Regarding the programme content: what are the lines that Peter Hall is pursuing and how can the programme reflect them? I get drawn in. An audience would be helped through the dense factual detail in the play by a family tree of its characters and a map highlighting where events took place. I feel sure that Hall would want to include appropriate quotations from Harley Granville Barker, whose vision he obviously shares; these would also provide the rationale behind the sixteenth-century/classical design of the production. Because the maturity of Antony and Cleopatra is central to this production, I suggest that their vast experience and ambition, prior to the action of the play, should be conveyed – and am asked to write a piece to this effect. For the main article, an approach is made to Anne Barton, professor of English at Cambridge University and a brilliant writer on sixteenth- and seventeenth-century drama.

To produce my five hundred words, I need to do considerable background research on Roman/Egyptian history of the first century BC, which adds enormously to my appreciation of the play. Since so much factual detail is impacted in Shakespeare's text, I feel that knowledge about the period has a validity not always applicable to a creative work. I suddenly understand the resonance of Parthia, for instance, where Marcus Crassus suffered one of the most disastrous defeats in Roman history in 53 BC. Since this blocked expansion of the Empire to the east, Ventidius (in the play) has real cause to be wary of Antony's envy when he defeats the Parthians in his leader's place.

Alexandria was a sophisticated city of architectural splendour, centre of scientific, philosophic and cultural development, at a time when Rome was still somewhat provincial and rough-hewn, focused on martial expansion: if one knows more about the two worlds straddled by the play, the culture clash between its Egyptian and Roman characters gains in texture.

To learn that the Romans had an age-old mistrust of the sea, and that Antony's genius as a warrior was only for fighting on land, gives one a greater understanding of the military action in the play, and of the gambling element in Antony's character.

Cleopatra's background before she met Antony throws light on what she stands to gain politically by her involvement with him – and how much she stands to lose by Octavius Caesar's ascendancy.

NOTES FOR THE PROGRAMME:

By the time of Antony and Cleopatra's encounter upon the river Cydnus, both of them were aged in the ways of the world, vastly experienced, supremely ambitious.

Cleopatra VII, a Macedonian descended from one of Alexander the Great's generals, Ptolemy I, was queen of the richest country in the Mediterranean, and had learned early the hardships of power in a court riddled with corruption, intrigue, family violence and murder (engendered by Pharaoh-style incestuous marriages). The Ptolemaic dynasty was threatened with extinction by the encroaching Roman Empire: her weak, dissolute father, caused to flee Egypt by a restive populace, had been reinstated by Roman forces (led by a brilliant young cavalry officer who was said to be impressed by the fourteen-year-old Cleopatra's wit and beauty; his name was Mark Antony). Once Queen, she too was in exile, preparing to wage war on her brother-husband, when Julius Caesar, conqueror of half the world, arrived in the East. She became his mistress, bore him a son, Caesarion, and followed him to Rome – potential mistress of the world. When he was assassinated she returned to Egypt to await developments.

Mark Antony, too, had covered a lot of ground. The finest Roman general after Caesar, he had been with him in Gaul and supported him against Pompey the Great in Greece. The archetypal hardened soldier, handsome, virile, loved by his men and the common people for his open nature and generosity, he was also (in the words of Renan), 'a colossal child, capable of conquering the world but incapable of resisting a pleasure' – extravagant, a great womanizer and excessive drinker. He had the emotional, political and military control of Rome at Caesar's death. However, the latter's will named his great-nephew, Octavius, as heir, adopting him into the Julian family. To avoid civil war, a Triumvirate of Octavius, Antony and Lepidus was formed, dividing the rule of the Empire among them. An indiscriminate orgy of murder against Caesar's conspirators climaxed with Antony as hero of Philippi, where the last of them were wiped out. A triumphal tour of the East followed, with Antony hailed as conqueror, the new Caesar, Hercules. . . .

He seemed destined to take over as sole master of the Roman world, and, summoned to Tarsus as queen of a client-state, in the late summer of 41 BC, Cleopatra set out to seduce him, both with her consummate femininity (Plutarch: 'So sweete was her companie and conversacion, that a man could not possibly but be taken') and the infinite refinements of pleasure the Hellenistic-Egyptian world had evolved. The attraction between such glamorous, powerful beings was inevitable: both had loved before, but in this union lay the last, the supreme chance to fulfil every personal and political aspiration.

According to a popular saying, it was 'Aphrodite come to revel with Dionysus for the good of Asia', glorious – and doomed.

This is, of course, history become mythology: Shakespeare shows that their excesses caused them to misuse their accumulated experience, and err seriously in their judgement. Hall: 'The greatest soldier in the world is a fool – drunk and dissolute, whilst Egypt's Queen, the great enchantress, is actually a scheming strumpet.'

OTHER BIOGRAPHIES

OCTAVIUS, who had fought with Caesar in Spain, was named his heir and adopted son in the assassinated man's will. Brought up in the country, quiet, studious and often ill, he gradually revealed a political brilliance and unswerving ambition equal to Caesar's own. The Triumvirate's formation gave him Africa, Sicily and Sardinia and (with Antony in the East, Lepidus in the West) effective control of Italy. When the pact with Pompey broke down, Octavius routed him from the Mediterranean, thanks to his brilliant right-hand man, Agrippa. Similarly, he got rid of Lepidus who attempted to challenge him. The breakdown of his sister Octavia's marriage to Antony provided his justification for confronting the last obstacle to total control of the Roman Empire, and the battle of Actium and subsequent deaths of Antony and Cleopatra gained him Egypt and its wealth. Given the honoured title Augustus, as peacebringer, social, legal and commercial reformer, he turned the vestiges of the Republic into a dictatorship and was declared a god at his death.

LEPIDUS, a governor of Hither Spain, supported Antony at Julius Caesar's death, to be appointed to the Triumvirate as buffer between the conflicting ambitions of the other two. He was only interested in preserving peace to keep his own weak head above water. He played an independent part in the campaign against Sextus Pompey and was then unwise enough to lay claim to Sicily, for which Octavius forced him to retire to his home near Naples, where he spent his last twenty-five years.

SEXTUS POMPEY was the younger son of Pompey the Great, whom Julius Caesar defeated in Thessaly. (His older brother was the

Pompey received by Cleopatra.) After his father's murder, he won successes against the governors of Further Spain, backed by Pompeian fugitives. On Caesar's death, the Senate appointed him commander of the fleet but then outlawed, he used Sicily as a base for raiding and blockading the Italian coast. (A continuing grievance was that Antony acquired and despoiled Pompey the Great's splendid town house in Rome.) The Treaty of Misenum was patched up with the Triumvirate, but Pompey went back to piracy, strutting around in green robes, posing as the son of Neptune. Eventually defeated by Octavius' general Agrippa, he escaped to Asia Minor, there to be captured and executed by Antony's men.

OCTAVIA, Octavius' sister, widow of Caius Marcellus, married Antony and spent several years with him in Athens. A Roman matron of virtue and intelligence, her diplomacy brought about the Treaty of Tarentum, temporarily reconciling husband and brother. Dismissed to Rome when pregnant with their second daughter, she sent Antony supplies and 2,000 men (which he rejected) for his intended campaign against Parthia. Despite his reunion with Cleopatra and Octavius' wish to capitalize on the wrong she had been done, she remained in Antony's house in Rome, even once he had formally divorced her, receiving and assisting his envoys and caring not only for her own children but for those by his marriage to Fulvia. She won universal esteem for her nobility and humanity.

Many of the actors, too, have been doing background reading. Obviously, anything which contradicts or is foisted upon the play does it disservice. But the history I have read helps to clarify the text. If the actors know as much as possible about their characters and the period, surely it will contribute to the 'layering' of their performances?

Tim Pigott-Smith puzzles over how to communicate information gleaned not from the text but from background research: how, for example, does he convey Octavius' anxiety about his political position, that he is Julius Caesar's *adoptive* son whose assumed mantle of power is thus precarious?

Of course, he cannot be specific. But if in general he interprets the text in the light of his additional knowledge, something subliminal will communicate itself to the audience. Ultimately they will receive an enriched and holistic view of Octavius, in which underlying anxiety has meshed with the other facets of his personality. Exact historical sources become unimportant.

Judi Dench had been delighted to discover that when Antony returned to Rome, Cleopatra was carrying twins, born just before his marriage to Octavia. She felt it put everything into perspective. Certainly the words in their parting scene assumed a new loading – 'The sides of nature/Will not sustain it', 'What says the married woman' and even 'Cut my lace, Charmian'.

Peter Hall smiles enigmatically: 'It's not in Shakespeare.' He has a resistance to extraneous information which might give implications to the text which the writer had not intended. When, after weekends, he talks of having done 'a lot of homework', he means he had dug further into *Antony and Cleopatra* itself or re-read *Julius Caesar*, North's Plutarch translation or Granville Barker. I understand this resistance as far as Cleopatra's pregnancy is concerned – Shakespeare would have referred to so significant a circumstance if he had wanted it included in our thinking – but in general I am puzzled by it.

Watching the play in the final weeks of rehearsal, I realize that Hall has arrived at exactly the same conclusions that historical research would have provided. This confirms, tangibly, the enormous richness and subtlety of the writing and the director's capacity to mine it. Whatever is not stated factually emerges through speech patterns, key words, character complexity, action and reaction. It truly is all there – in the play itself and mostly 'on the line'.

CHAPTER 6

Character, Problem Scenes, Action!

Character

The story of the play has been traced, by questioning the function of each scene, and how best to communicate it. By now, too, through a blend of imaginative projection and intellect, most of the actors have begun to make real connections with their roles, large or small. By laying in a rich store of insights, they are moving towards such identification with character as to know his or her range of responses to any given situation.

What path do these responses follow? In parallel with the company quest for a line through the narrative, each actor must find the through-line of his own character's behaviour. As ever, the clues are in the text. Hence the probing: 'Why do I say this? How does it connect with what I said or did before?' Individual interpretation will be shaped by and, in turn, will shape the production as a whole.

The play is vividly coloured by the massive inconsistencies of its two central characters: Cleopatra is mercurial, perverse and quixotic, rising to a 'marble constant' and noble end, whilst Antony is a man of passion bursting the bounds of Roman stoicism. Inconsistent though they may be, it is important that Dench and Hopkins, playing them, find a logic behind the leaps from one mood or mode of behaviour to another, and so deeply digest the connecting factors as to make them intelligible – and credible – to an audience.

This applies to other characters. For Tim Pigott-Smith, the excitement in Shakespeare arises from the ambiguities. Thus Caesar is capable of genuine affection for his sister and, while condemning Antony's 'wassails', can yet feel awed admiration for his heroism as a soldier and be moved to tears at his death. Enobarbus, who poses as a cynical mysogynist –

Under a compelling occasion, let women die.
It were pity to cast them away for nothing though
between them and a great cause they should be esteemed
nothing.

– voices the most exquisite appreciation of Cleopatra and the femininity she embodies; he, of all people, dies of a broken heart.

Obviously choices will have to be made, with director and fellow
actors as sounding board. As in real life, a character could have a
variety of reactions to a situation. The choice settled on is not
arbitrary but dependent on how it best slots into the context: unlike
real life, the actor knows where his story is going and how it ends.

From quite early on, Judi Dench has happily anticipated that no two
performances with Antony Hopkins will be alike. He revels in taking
different paths to the same conclusion, and makes full use of
rehearsals to experiment with this. In one run-through he starts off
relaxed, too relaxed, a wine glass always to hand, even sucking a
sweet whilst politicking with Caesar. Although the charm and
confidence work well in the optimistic first section of the play, they
run him into trouble later. He has not released sufficient of Antony's
grandeur and command, for his fall from power *over half the world* to
seem momentous. It is a question of giving himself a high enough
plateau to fall *from* – pitching the performance so as to incorporate all
its dimensions.

In the first two scenes of the play, we get the two sides of Antony:
in Alexandria, he has been free to live by his senses, indulging his
passion and his pleasure. For him to say, publicly:

Let Rome in Tiber melt and the wide arch
Of the ranged empire fall:

is as if he would shed all the Roman values he believes in – here is the
recklessness and lack of judgement which will destroy him. In the
following scene, he comes to his senses. Italy is riddled with strife
and his wife is dead:

I must from this enchanting queen break off.

When Enobarbus enters, the dialogue between Hopkins and
Bryant becomes quite specific: Antony's presence must be such as to
re-establish command, and his rank over Enobarbus. Hopkins'

speech is crisp and authoritative – Antony as sober leader returning to the service of his Empire. Michael Bryant pursues the familiar, joking vein they would have fallen into during their sojourn in Egypt. (In this scene alone, he has found most of the clues to his character: the bluff old cynic who is, in fact, deeply sensitive but works hard to conceal it.)

The relationship between the two men is shown as it was and, sharply, as it is now – and is echoed in the scene of their return to Rome, when Antony silences his companion during the conference with Caesar and Lepidus:

> Thou art a soldier only. Speak no more.

Enobarbus' reply: 'Go to then: your considerate stone', invariably raises a laugh.

(Like the character he plays, Bryant keeps up a flow of dry asides. He compares Antony's decryal of:

> Our slippery people
> Whose love is never linked to the deserver
> Till his deserts are past,

to 'the critics giving us bad notices all our lives, then writing an obituary on "the great loss to British theatre of this superb actor"'.)

Hopkins carries the control of this scene over to Antony's reactions to Cleopatra in the next. He tries to break the news of his departure gently and, as she continues to mock his honour, interrupts with facts, expressed jagged and staccato, imprisoning her arms to enforce her attention:

> Hear me Queen:
> The strong necessity of time commands
> Our services awhile. . . .
> . . . . Our Italy
> Shines o'er with civil swords. Sextus Pompeius
> Makes his approaches to the port of Rome.

When she chooses to use even news of Fulvia's death against him, his anger mounts. Hopkins: 'I can only stand quite still, or else I'd hit her.' Because she changes tack and cheers him on his honourable way, they are warmly reconciled (he standing behind Dench, embracing her whilst they speak out front) – but it is a far cry from the carefree passion of the first scene. Roman thoughts have conquered.

When not in a scene, Judi Dench sits quietly in a corner, blocking out distraction as she studies her lines. Wholly still and focused, she brings the same quality of concentration onstage, to connect with each switch of Cleopatra's mood: when Antony tells her Fulvia is dead, she twirls in scarce-hidden delight, then builds up a storm of self-pity, flinging away the letter carrying the news, making zig-zag forays of rage to and away from him:

> Now I see, I see
> In Fulvia's death, how mine received shall be.

Realizing she may have gone too far, she melts into submissiveness: she may not be able to stop him going, but she can counter the pull of Rome by 'conquering in retreat'.

There is a desolation at the heart of the self-dramatizing: Dench has talked of Cleopatra's awareness that this is the last great passion of her life (comparing her with Beatrice in *Much Ado About Nothing*: 'If she and Benedict didn't get together in that last summer, then there was no hope. . . .'). In the later scene when she disposes of:

> My salad days,
> When I was green in judgement, cold in blood . . .

there is a darkness, a bitterness, almost (at this final chance for love), which Hall catches at: 'You had it, Judi! Build on that.' He refers to 'menopausal love', the evidence that Cleopatra was already middle-aged: 'her waned lip', 'age cannot wither her' (i.e. an age already arrived at), her reference to herself as 'wrinkled deep in time' and the long pause when she hears that Octavia is (only) thirty, all of which the actress digests. A growing element of desperation will suffuse Cleopatra's hold over Antony. He is the centre of her world, the force round which she circles, reacting, play-acting, to his every mood:

> If you find him sad,
> Say I am dancing, if in mirth, report
> That I am sudden sick.

To Dench, Hall says of Cleopatra's perversity and mercurial switches: 'You shouldn't ever let them get a single idea of her.' To Hopkins, 'You don't have to play the whole man in every scene.' It seems an exact appraisal of the different 'rhythms' at which their temperaments operate.

Day by day, Judi Dench is absorbing the many facets of the character and tapping her own qualities to give them substance: the energy, the quick intelligence and wit, the 'gutsiness', the femininity, the playfulness, the authority, the pensiveness and vulnerability. Both on and offstage, a warm relationship with Cleopatra's entourage has developed (and it is not surprising to learn, later, that it is with the Cleopatra who had the common touch and inspired great loyalty, the Cleopatra whom Enobarbus once saw 'Hop forty paces through the public street', that Dench most closely identifies).

Her movements are becoming feline, as she prowls and wheels. On the attack, she is like a darting cobra. She takes some convincing by Hall that her many entrances 'sweeping through those doors' will not be dull. Each is, in fact, arresting, as she possesses the stage in a new and unpredictable mood: she throws herself to the ground and stretches full-length for 'Give me to drink mandragora', evoking a heat-induced lethargy (Act I Scene 5). One feels the brooding restlessness of 'Give me some music . . . Let it alone! Let's to billiards', which will erupt into her attack on the Messenger/Eros (Act II Scene 5) and the impatience of the jealous mistress who wants to cross-examine him about Octavia – 'Where is the fellow?' – in Act III Scene 3.

Within each scene is a whole range of colourings: the barbed digs at Mardian, full of sexual innuendo, ripen into blatant sexual longing, as she curls up with her head in Charmian's lap: 'O happy horse, to bear the weight of Antony!' She radiates joy when Alexas brings a message from him (which she leans forward to hear whilst her women examine the pearl ring he has sent, on her outstretched hand). The venom with which she lashes out at Charmian for teasing her about Julius Caesar is capped by the glee of a tyrant at her capacity to 'unpeople Egypt'. An infatuated woman then races off happily, to write to her lover.

In Act II Scene 5, she has entered morose and irritable, her court lurking by the door, wary of her caprices, hoping she will find something to amuse her. Charmian runs forward to share the intimate reminiscence of:

> that night
> I laughed him into patience; and next morn

> Ere the ninth hour, I drunk him to his bed:
> Then put my tires and mantles on him, whilst
> I wore his sword Philippan.

The rest keep well back, terrified of her fury against the bearer of bad tidings (Eros) on whom she draws a knife (afterwards making as if to throttle Charmian who has dared to defend him). A moment of sad self-awareness:

> These hands do lack nobility, that they strike
> A meaner than myself . . .

is followed by Dench's ironic interpretation of:

> Though it be honest, it is never good
> To bring bad news . . .

but in the catch of her darkened, husky voice, as she repeats 'He is married?', and until the end of the scene, is the full weight of Cleopatra's despair. In a later rehearsal Dench introduces a vocal block in pronouncing 'Octavia', as if the word chokes her. In the final speech, she hurls herself into Charmian's protective arms with a full-throated howl of pain; it is both child-like and animal.

When Cleopatra recalls the Messenger in Act III Scene 3, Dench shows her self-possession and imperiousness apparently restored. She fires off a series of questions about Antony's new wife and seems to be delighted with the answers (or at least the interpretation she puts upon them). However, the forlorn aside contained in:

> That Herod's head
> I'll have; but how, when Antony is gone,
> Through whom I might command it?

establishes an undercurrent of anxiety, held throughout the scene by Charmian's over-rapid responses:

CLEOPATRA   . . . He cannot like her long.
CHARMIAN   Like her? O Isis! 'Tis impossible.

CLEOPATRA   The man hath seen some majesty and should
                                                                know.
CHARMIAN   Hath he seen majesty? . . .

Her court shadow Cleopatra's every move, including crowding in behind her like a flock of birds when, dignity shaken, she rushes for the door on hearing that Octavia is younger than she. They have suffered with her through her present grief, admire her courage – and will die with her at the play's end. (Peter Hall: 'All of this would have had special meaning for Shakespeare's audience. Elizabeth I, when raddled with age, was still treated by her devoted court as though she was young and desirable.')

The actors extract every comic inflection from the scene. Hall's detailed direction does not let them – or us – lose sight of its haunting poignancy, the reality of the mistress displaced by the wife.

In many ways, the small roles are more difficult than the large: to develop a character (and not merely an outline caricature), from a handful of lines, requires imagination and skill. To stand around through scene after scene, as do the actors who make up Cleopatra's entourage, is a supreme test of concentration: their roles are largely built on silent reaction. Yet there is definition: they each observe their mistress and bend to her whims in different ways. Miranda Foster's Charmian is flirtatious, eyeing visiting Romans but, above all, tenderly maternal towards Cleopatra, sensitive to her moods, sharing her pain and risking her anger to give her advice. The Iras of Helen Fitzgerald is delicate, more reticent. Iain Ormsby-Knox plays Mardian so that one feels for his cautious dignity and Frances Quinn (as a non-speaking attendant) has a smiling sensuousness. Bob Arnold, an actor of sensitivity and warmth, has made Alexas into a charming courtier, an Elizabethan gallant. (Of Jerry Flynn's slowly but surely emerging Eros, more later.)

Working on the Soothsayer scene, Peter Hall challenges the women's capacity to extend their boundaries: 'You've got to be more abandoned, wilder, cheekier. Make it more raunchy, Miranda, sharper and wittier, Helen.' To Dan Thorndike: 'You're playing it old. Don't. Take your time, give it more gravity.' (To an extent, the actor is 'working against type': the Soothsayer needs a detached, menacing quality, foreign to Thorndike's gentle responsiveness.)

This scene is problematic: the women hear something disturbing – their fortunes are alike and, ominously, the best is behind them. Although they interpret it lightly, the seriousness of the Soothsayer's forecasts must be well-planted, for Shakespeare is laying a trail to what lies ahead.

Introducing this as early as the second scene in the play, he must have believed that his audience knew the outcome of the tragedy – or were able to recall the auguries when they were borne out, almost four hours later, in the final scene. To digress for a moment: after weeks of exposure to *Antony and Cleopatra*, I have a growing conviction that he would not have spilled such a wealth of factual detail on spectators who had no framework for it. The fate of Charmian and Iras *would* have been known. When North's translation of Plutarch appeared in 1579, although the events themselves had occurred sixteen hundred years before, I believe they became as much the subject for speculation, gossipy and philosophical, as any political scandal of today. Indeed, history as a moral example, but examined as if current. Is it fanciful to think that where we, the recipients of overmuch data, are trapped in structured concepts of time and place, the Elizabethans, being less encumbered, straddled distance with flexible imagination – and so made the past their own? Granville Barker's ideas on Elizabethan staging would seem to bear this out.

As to Elizabethan memory: it is on record that the first performance of *Hamlet* in Africa was in 1603. This was by a ship's crew some of whom had seen the play in London the previous summer. On the voyage out, they amused themselves by piecing it together *from memory*, then staged it in its entirety once they landed. Again, the numerous Messengers in Shakespeare parody fact: tracts of detailed information, in verse, were conveyed verbally by emissaries who had memorized them, and often spent weeks or months reaching their destinations. In both these cases, the structure and devices of verse were a vital aid to memory. Predating literacy, the oral tradition lingered. The spoken word was retained. Therefore, in the dénouement of *Antony and Cleopatra*, an Elizabethan audience would have heard echoes of the Soothsayer's warnings in Scene 2 with a cathartic sense of coming full circle.

Back in the rehearsal room, the staging of this scene opens out, to allow more movement. As a focus, a crystal ball is introduced; when Miranda Foster snatches it from Thorndike, the gesture is aptly outrageous – she seems to be playing with her destiny.

I find it interesting that, as character becomes defined and as language is used with precise understanding and greater relish, external ballast begins to disappear. The cushions and rugs have gone from the Soothsayer and Cleopatra scenes, as has the table from the conference scenes in Rome.

Movement of the door and wall-sections will be much reduced over the ensuing weeks; when they *are* moved, the effect is potent. There is an inevitable progression from complexity to simplicity, from props and set as appendages to that which is starkly symbolic and reinforces the text. In Pompey's first scene, stools had been introduced, on which his guerrilla band sat drinking. Hall then decided that this did not sufficiently tell the story: Pompey is denying war whilst his followers warn him of its imminence. The stools are discarded, to be replaced by a rack upstage, against which the machinery of war – weapons and shields – is relentlessly piled, contrapuntal to the leader's downstage preening. In every respect, rehearsals have become a process of selection.

Tim Pigott-Smith, having done further homework on Octavius Caesar's background, wants to point up his relative youth, in comparison to Antony, his inexperience and bookishness. Therefore, at the first appearance of himself and Lepidus (Act I Scene 4), he has introduced qualities which convey this: his Caesar is obviously unsure of himself and of the correct posture to strike. He overdoes the self-righteous indignation at Antony's dalliance in Alexandria, trying to engage Lepidus in a shared anger that they should 'bear/So great weight in his lightness'. An influx of messengers bringing news of danger on 'The borders maritime' from Pompey and his piratical allies makes him noticeably nervous. As he voices a novice's admiration for Antony's prowess as an old campaigner, one detects a strong element of hero worship. He longs for Antony's arrival, whilst affecting sternness:

> Let his shames quickly
> Drive him to Rome.

Meanwhile, he champs at the bit: he and Lepidus should make a move to quell Pompey.

Of Lepidus, Peter Hall has warned of 'the danger of taking him too lightly, of playing his end – when he was stripped of office – too soon'. His presence, albeit hollow, must be substantial enough to make it credible that he was appointed a Triumvir. In this scene,

Octavius obviously needs his elder statesmanship. In fleshing out a character written somewhat monochromatically, John Bluthal uses self-important gestures and a mellow, conciliatory tone: his Lepidus takes on weight and expansiveness.

Having dispensed with the conference table, they now also 'strike' the three chairs and the actors move around freely as they speak. No one is satisfied. Pigott-Smith in particular feels the difficulty of conveying information 'about which a modern audience has no prior knowledge, in language which is sometimes so densely impacted as to be hard to grasp in the reading, let alone when heard'. (Again, I am reminded of Hall's observation about the decreasing likelihood of this language being intelligible to audiences of the future.) By making the scene obviously 'public' – reinstating the emblematic Triumviral chairs and having several soldiers stand to attention in the background – these chairs become anchors from which the actors can present their arguments, holding our attention by words alone without the distraction of movement. Pigott-Smith sits until impelled to rise by:

> 'Tis time we twain
> Did show ourselves i'th'field. . . .

The actors' enhanced understanding of their characters, both internally and in relation to the development of the play, carries over to the conference scene, once Antony arrives in Rome. Here he is at his most able, the seasoned statesman. He hopes to redeem himself and will listen to and deal with complaints, even 'play the penitent' up to a point. Tim Pigott-Smith, whom we had seen noisy with recriminations behind Antony's back, now shows a Caesar initially intimidated in his hero's presence, petulant and hurt:

> I wrote to you
> When, rioting in Alexandria, you
> Did pocket up my letters. . . .

Political inexperience leads him to overstep the mark: he accuses Antony of breaking 'the article of your oath'. At this, the atmosphere freezes. Antony's honour, of which he is fiercely protective, is being questioned. Bluthal, as peace-keeping chairman, interposes bland, soothing comments. Caesar's vulnerability is exposed; without Antony's support, he is helpless:

> Yet if I knew
> What hoop should hold us staunch. . . .

In response, Agrippa (Basil Henson) steps forward, and in severe, measured tones suggests the marriage between Antony and Octavia. Pigott-Smith: 'And I'm trapped! I'll have to sacrifice my sister to this womanizer . . . which would explain my later anxiety in parting from her.'

Hall encourages the actors to have the confidence to take the scene slowly, allowing the force of arguments, spoken and tacit, to surface. It has a muscularity which they can all get their teeth into: they savour the lines and the brinkmanship involved in the negotiations.

Problem Scenes

The length of the rehearsal period determines the pacing of the work and, of course, the amount of detail in the finished product. In this sixth week (with seven weeks still to go before the play opens) the atmosphere is unpressurized and creatively liberating. New elements are introduced each time a scene is re-run, and reinforced the next time round. But there is also time for complete reappraisal as insights deepen. On some scenes, particularly, the director and cast experiment continuously, trying to find a staging that will give the maximum clarity and dramatic value to the interpretation of the lines.

The confrontation between the Triumvirate and Pompey (Act II Scene 6) has, Hall feels, become too explicit: 'I'm sure this scene is about politicians who never say what they are thinking. The underlying irony gives it a richness. Conceal your hostility beneath a veil of utmost charm. Make it sound perfectly genuine. The art is to show how "nice" you can be.'

David Schofield, keeping in mind an image of Mussolini, struts and flourishes, airing his grievances. Pompey the Great is called upon as a sanction; his son blockaded Italy

> To scourge th' ingratitude that despiteful Rome
> Cast on my noble father.

Julius Caesar had been assassinated because he aspired to kingship: yet here are the Triumvirate setting themselves up as gods – and he has pettier complaints. Where Hopkins, Pigott-Smith and Bluthal had previously squared up to him in playing the scene, they now collude in being placatory. Even his barbed references to Cleopatra are taken smilingly. The martial event becomes an elaborate and face-saving dance towards concluding an advantageous treaty.

As they go off to celebrate their entente cordiale, the honest exchange between Enobarbus and Menas is in pointed contrast to the hypocrisy we have just witnessed. Michael Bryant and Michael Carter play it with cynical humour.

The irony continues in the banquet scene on Pompey's galley. Pompey's sailors and servants stand waiting to bow the great ones in, a fanfare of trumpets will sound – and then the drunken, slurring, staggering 'pillars of the earth' enter. Servants carry in the food, top up the wine. In the midst of the revelry of this brotherly mob, Menas takes Pompey aside to offer to cut the throats of the 'three world-sharers' and so leave Pompey 'lord of all the world'. Invoking a distorted notion of honour, the latter regrets

> Being done unknown
> I should have found it afterwards well done,
> But must condemn it now. . . .

Lepidus is carried away drunk. Enobarbus raises a frisson by addressing Antony as 'emperor'. . . . Pompey again refers to Antony's possession of his father's house. . . . At the end of the scene, when Menas, in a gesture of scorn, has the trumpets sounded for 'these great fellows', it expresses a disgust the audience should feel: these political giants are nothing but *mafiosi*, dangerous opportunists.

Hall warns against an indiscriminate drunkenness: each actor must hold his liquor – or not – in character. Menas very sober and precise in contrast to the 'piss-artistry' in the background. 'Let's play it less woolly, harder. You should all be working on how you can score off each other.'

(Investigation of the above scenes – 6 and 7 in Act II – is obsessively pursued. Then, in the tenth week of rehearsal, working in the Olivier itself, Hall will seize the opportunities afforded by the auditorium and vast expanse of the stage and restage both.)

The opening of Act III Scene 2 refers back to the banquet scene.

Enobarbus and Agrippa's mockery of Lepidus has the queasiness of a hangover. Agrippa is slightly smug at having pulled off the reconciliation between Antony and Octavius. Enobarbus is dismayed that Antony has compromised himself. How Lepidus relates to his fellow Triumvirs ('They are his shards and he is their beetle') is visually carried through when the threesome enters, with Bluthal flanked by Hopkins and Pigott-Smith. Sally Dexter follows; we have already heard that Octavia has been weeping at the prospect of leaving Rome.

The ensuing scene is one of those which proves troublesome and continues so for the next month. What has seemed simple becomes a morass of complexity. Everyone has a different theory, an alternative solution, and these threaten to bury the storyline completely.

Peter Hall: 'This scene is a "plant". The framework of a relationship must be set up so that there is one to be broken later.' Although he made the marriage for political reasons, Antony feels a tenderness for Octavia. He and Caesar are apparently united. Caesar, meanwhile, feels a great deal for his sister, at the same time as having his political aims served by her marriage, and she, Octavia, is both the stoic Roman matron, well aware of the politics of power, and the anxious woman going off to a strange country with a man who has the reputation of a libertine. Small wonder she is torn, in Antony's gentle words:

> . . . . the swan's-down feather
> That stands upon the swell at the full of tide
> And neither way inclines.

The difficulty, then, is that each character has to steer a path between his or her conflicting emotions. Hall warns Dexter against overplaying the regret and pain of parting: 'If you start off in an over-hesitant mood, you somehow let the air out. . . .'

Several weeks later, through a subtle orchestration of movement which mirrors each nuance of feeling, the scene is at last unlocked. It becomes poignant and defined; Octavia, her back to the audience, crouches down in the space between her husband and her brother, as if she can no longer withstand the choices imposed upon her. When she moves to cling to Caesar, his rigid constraint gives way: he has to fight back his tears. Impatient at the prolonged leave-taking, Antony separates them by drawing Caesar into a brisk bear-hug – 'Look, here I have you; thus I let you go' – from which the latter visibly shrinks. (As a foil to the easy physicality of Hopkins' Antony, Pigott-Smith is building Caesar's frigidity into the way he hesitates before a handshake, recoils from an embrace.)

Lepidus moves in to kiss Octavia's hand, and, before any further emotion can well up, Antony virtually yanks her off stage. One wonders how long his sympathy for her will last.

Building on what has been established in this scene, when they go into its follow-up (Act III Scene 4), Hall thinks this through with great delicacy with the actors: 'Sally, you don't dare come any closer to Antony. . . . Tony, can you bear to have her touch you? The dead marriage. You're full of regret and bitterness.' Hopkins must make each accusation against Caesar top the one before. Octavia's lines are 'as close to an emotional appeal as this stoical lady ever gets. We must feel the pain beneath her restraint,' says Hall. In the rhythm of the play this is a slow, black scene.

It is in this sixth week that Hall finally reaches a decision on the placing of the interval. In the process of rehearsing, it has become obvious that the play has two quite defined movements – the period when Antony is in the ascendant, confident of success in everything he touches, followed by the downfall and suicide of him and Cleopatra. The turning point in their fortunes is their defeat at the battle of Actium.

Ending Part One at Act III Scene 6 will leave it at a point of explosion: we see the causes for civil war in Caesar's reaction to Antony's desertion of Octavia. After the interval, Act III Scene 7 is in dramatic counterpoint: we see Antony reunited with Cleopatra, their preparation for battle and, significantly, Antony's first major error of tactics – his decision to fight by sea. As with the emergent clarity of so much else, the interval break now seems surprisingly self-evident, in terms of the narrative, the build-up of dramatic tension, the strength of the opening of the second half and, not least, the timing: Part One will run approximately 1 hour 40 minutes, Part Two, about 1 hour 50.

Decision made, the scenes abutting the interval must now be tuned up, so that the play sustains the twenty-minute break, and rapidly re-engages the audience after it.

Act III Scene 6, then. Having got rid of Lepidus, Octavius now has full authority in Rome. Hall: 'It could be very eloquent to have his single chair onstage. . . .' It is, and again the chair provides an anchor from which Tim Pigott-Smith can convey a wad of information: Cleopatra and Antony, in gilded magnificence (she dressed as the goddess Isis), have displayed themselves publicly in Alexandria, surrounded by 'Caesarion whom they call my father's son' and their illegitimate children. By calling his sons 'the kings of kings', as if to proclaim a dynasty, and dividing his portion of the Empire between them and Cleopatra, Antony has insulted Rome, his motherland and its gods.

The status of Caesarion is an insult and threat to Octavius' own lineage: 'Issue that line as a challenge,' says Hall. Otherwise, since Caesar's objective is to provoke a sense of outrage in his listeners, Agrippa and Maecenas, he suggests that the lines be delivered as plain facts. Divested of emotion, they are chillingly effective. In reply to accusations from Antony, Caesar's

> I have told him Lepidus had grown too cruel,
> That he his high authority abused
> And did deserve his change

is, in Hall's words, 'a wonderful Stalinist line'. As Pigott-Smith plays him, Caesar is developing into the steely manipulator who will dispose of every obstacle on his way to absolute power (thus becoming the Augustus Caesar of history, who went on to rule the Empire for thirty years). A watchful tension and assurance has replaced the insecurity Caesar had displayed in earlier scenes.

Pigott-Smith is downstage centre, his back to the audience, when Octavia appears upstage, facing him. Only now does he give rein to pent-up anger, as emotion for his sister fuses with his desire for revenge. Antony has betrayed them both:

> . . . let determined things to destiny
> Hold unbewailed their way.

Octavia succumbs to the inevitability of war and finally moves into her brother's enfolding arms. With the play firmly braced for the struggle to come, the lights will dim to black-out.

Establishing the tone with which the play will resume in Act III Scene 7, Judi Dench says crisply: 'Since you last saw us, Antony and I have made ourselves Emperor and Empress so we must start off very high, very self-assured – then our downfall will seem even greater. Would this be in the war office?' Hall: 'We'll make the statement by having Enobarbus and Antony's general, Canidius, come on in armour.' Dench: 'And I'm wearing a very nice war-coat. . . .'

Again, Peter Hall has been digging into the text for clues: 'In the first half of the play, Cleopatra was unsure of her hold over Antony: there was his wife Fulvia, he was away from Egypt for a long time, and married Octavia. But in the second half, her sexuality has triumphed. Antony has come back to her and very publicly declared Alexandria as his new power-base, effectively destroying his allegiance to the Triumvirate. So, from now on, she is in the ascendant over Antony who never does anything without consulting her – he is truly what they say he is: "Manned by a woman". And Enobarbus watches all this and is worried stiff. . . .

'There is also some area of strain between them which is going to lead him to turn against her with great resentment later. He has to keep proving himself. He wouldn't dare refuse to fight by sea at Actium; in Jungian terms she is sea and moon – it would be like refusing to go to bed with her. It's a sexual challenge, almost.'

(This is a prime example of Hall having made deductions from the text which accord completely with historical evidence: Cleopatra seems to have insisted on a legal marriage to Antony and made him recognize Caesarion as heir to the Empire. It was probably at her insistence that the provocative Triumph was staged in Alexandria. In addition, the great warrior was now forced to depend on the assistance of a woman for his military campaigns: it was she who supplied the Egyptian fleet, and money for the troops, grain and arms needed at Actium, placing him overwhelmingly in her debt.)

Hall: 'You two are in cahoots about fighting at sea.' Dench: 'Ideally the others should come on as soldiers and we should be dressed as sailors?' Cleopatra is cool and resolved: she knows she has Antony in her pocket although she does not let him see it. Antony is somewhat high because he is frightened. Hall: 'As a pact communicates itself between the two, they actually turn their backs on Canidius and Enobarbus.'

When a Soldier (Mike Hayward) comes on to plead:

> . . . we
> Have been used to conquer standing on the earth
> And fighting foot to foot . . .

Antony bridles defensively – he knows his men are in the right.

In this 'axis' scene, two things have been accomplished: along with the forceful energy required to recall Part One and precipitate Part Two, important discords have been sounded, paving the way for what lies ahead.

They now do a run of Part One. What forcibly emerges for me is how often Shakespeare makes us juggle with double messages. Glints of trouble on the horizon, presages of doom, cast a shadow over surface evidence.

Enobarbus is the man who, although devoted to Antony, knows his weaknesses intimately: it is impossible to dismiss his cynical forecasts, even as we watch his master seemingly reformed. No sooner has Antony agreed to marry Octavia, than Enobarbus is reminding us of Cleopatra's endless fascination and (as Michael Bryant interprets it) snorting with laughter at the idea that Octavia's 'beauty, wisdom, modesty' will restrain him. In the next scene, the moment after Antony convinces us (and his bride-to-be) of his future fidelity, Shakespeare chooses to throw us into doubt again. The Soothsayer (travelled some way from Egypt!) provides Antony with justification for following his deepest inclinations:

> I will to Egypt
> And though I make this marriage for my peace,
> I'th'East my pleasure lies.

It is similarly unsettling when Enobarbus, alone with Menas, reports the marriage with assurances that, far from uniting Antony and Caesar, it will only serve to drive them apart: 'He will to his Egyptian dish again'. Throughout, the old cynic imposes a disturbing commentary on the action, which gnaws at our attention. (Later, of course, his gloomy and lucid rumblings do not allow a single tactical error, nor any stage in Antony's disintegration, to pass unnoticed.)

So although we may give a surface credence to the charade of Triumviral business – the patched-up brotherhood, the peace-making with Pompey, an initial kindness towards Octavia – we are gripped by the anticipation that Antony's addiction will finally throw his judgement.

As the play unfolds, scenes intercut between Rome and Egypt: we swing from 'masculine' stoicism to 'feminine' emotionalism, from preoccupation with matters military and political to obsession with love. Bridging the two, Antony and Enobarbus seem weighted with nostalgia for Alexandria (the latter openly rapturizing, the former suppressing a pensive sadness at every reference to Egypt). Within the Roman world it is a shock to go from the debauchery on Pompey's galley to the sombre scene of victory in Parthia (a contrast reinforced by Brian Spink's restrained and dignified Ventidius).

Peter Hall is pleased by the intact rhythm of Part One, in which scene follows scene in logical shape. However, he feels that the 'muscle' of individual scenes, which emerged when they were worked on in isolation, has become diffused in the run: 'The danger inherent in the short scenes in Shakespeare is that by the time you've found their colour, you're off. So you must bring it on with you. The *physical* life within each scene must be more eloquent, more fully stated: if you do it puritanically, you could end up as "talking heads". We must find the difference in movement between the Romans and the Egyptians. . . .'

It is left to the actors to deal with this contrast on their own.

Action!

Productions which include dance sequences will have a choreographer (and above Rehearsal Room 1 the cast of Lorca's *Yerma* start their day's work with the resounding practice of flamenco steps). For *Antony and Cleopatra*, however, there is a fight arranger: at the start of the seventh week, Malcolm Ranson ('Swords, knives, battle-axes, quarter-staffs, punch-ups, handbags . . .') comes in to assess the action problems of the play.

Everyone available – not excepting Sally Dexter, Frances Quinn, John Bluthal and David Schofield – has been drafted into the army. An afternoon is spent working on crowd scenes. Emma Lloyd shepherds groups to the appropriate area in the rehearsal room, and keeps track of halberds, banners and swords. Actors scribble notes for themselves – their points of entry and marching order. Peter Hall periodically refers to the model of the set and confers with his assistant Alan Cohen. Hands in pockets, springy on his feet, Ranson shakes his head: those straggling recruits will have to be *drilled*.

WEEK 7 – Wednesday 25 February

The company goes into the Olivier Theatre for the first time, to rehearse the battle sequences. Now that the enclosing 'fourth wall' of the rehearsal room has been replaced by the wide open spaces of the 1,100-seat auditorium, rising in raked curves before them, the actors adjust to the brightly-lit exposure with some self-consciousness. Joking and chatting, they stand around on stage, waiting to start. The screens and doors have been brought up by lift from the floor below; converging lines are taped on the stage. Action, which could only be approximated in the rehearsal room, opens out. There are unexpected distances to cross, not least from the 'slip' and upstage entrances to the central space of the stage. If one scene is to overlap with the next, so that this space never goes cold, entrances will have to be accurately timed and paced.

First, who amongst Caesar's army has a sense of rhythm? In consultation with composer Dominic Muldowney, a sturdy, bespectacled figure pacing the stalls, David Schofield and Simon Scott take up drums. Rolls reverberate round the theatre, as a cohort of banner-flourishing soldiers march after Taurus (Graham Sinclair), down the centre aisle of the stalls and up on to the stage. From the balcony overhanging stage right, Tim Pigott-Smith throws a scroll down to Sinclair, who catches it with aplomb. The army then moves off into the wings.

From a mere six lines of dialogue, Act III Scene 8 is filling out into a powerful display of military aggression. Two musician-drummers will later swell the ranks; Sinclair, 6' 3" tall, will assume fearsome proportions in a massive horned helmet, a black-strapped visor concealing his face.

Paul Arditti is on hand to assess the combination of sounds required for the sea battle of Actium, a noise which should flood the entire auditorium.

Now that they are in the theatre, the start of Act III Scene 11 can be released with full physical effect. Tony Hopkins runs through the auditorium, followed by his soldiers in disarray. They crouch in the aisles while he addresses them from the stage, isolated and confused by his first defeat. The impact is startling (and will be even more so in context, for until now in the play we will only have seen the self-assured extrovert):

> ANTONY   I am so lated in the world that I
> Have lost my way for ever. I have a ship
> Laden with gold; take that, divide it. Fly
> And make your peace with Caesar.
>
> ALL   Fly? Not we.

Hall coaches the group: 'Fly?' (*beat-beat*) 'Not we', so that they become a sorrowing chorus. Antony drives them off: 'Let that be left/Which leaves itself', repeating 'Friends be gone' until they gradually disappear up the aisle, appalled and silenced. Communicating a leaden despair, Hopkins then drops heavily to the ground.

After long runs of *Pravda* and *King Lear* in the same theatre, it is evident that he is completely at home in the Olivier. The husky voice and strong internal focus seem to pull the huge dimensions inwards. Pitched just above the conversational, his tone is wholly audible.

Good health and stamina are a prerequisite for an actor. For Hopkins and Judi Dench, carrying the burden of *Antony and Cleopatra* alongside their other taxing leading roles, there are obvious physical and mental pressures. Most of the company, rehearsing by day and playing in other productions at night, spend over twelve hours in the building, a warren of long corridors and rehearsal rooms which are artificially lit, ventilated and heated. A gymnasium existed but was swallowed up by the need for a second sound studio. There is no time to attend the dance and movement classes available at the NT Studio in the Old Vic annexe. The theatre's riverside location is useful for a quick stroll.

Often, at the end of a lunch break, they get rid of pent-up energy playing cricket in the rehearsal room – a Roman Seven v. an Alexandrian Six. Young Ian Bolt provides the commentary: 'The Man from the Book (Paul Greaves) comes in to bat . . . Dolabella throws the ball to Maecenas . . . a Poor Egyptian runs to catch it . . . and a cunning move from Caesar once again.'

Graham Sinclair refers to the 'show fitness' that results from a physically demanding production like *Animal Farm*. The perennial cigarette at his lips, Basil Henson talks critically of health conditions at the National: 'There's no doctor on the premises – but when do we have a chance to see one outside?' It says much for the commitment of a large cast that, in a thirteen-week period, only two of them have to take a day off through illness or injury.

CHAPTER 7

Reassessment and Challenges – The Layering Process

WEEKS 8/9/10 – Monday 2 March to
Saturday 21 March

Detailed work continues on Part Two of the play. As Peter Hall stands, glancing now at his script, now at the actors bringing it to life, the concentration in his tall figure, those hunched shoulders and heavy-lidded eyes, is enormous. He seems to be willing himself to hear the lines afresh each time they are re-run. Reappraised lines produce new and telling moves. . . .

In Act III Scene 11, as Antony sits on the ground and Cleopatra enters, supported by her women, Hall tells Hopkins to take:

> No, no, no, no, no . . .

slowly, each of them separated. It resounds like the toll of a funeral bell. He urges the others to use their half-lines, to fill the pauses after them. When Cleopatra is at last persuaded to move towards him, Dench lies full-length on the ground, face buried in her arms, shaken with weeping:

> O my lord, my lord,
> Forgive my fearful sails! I little thought
> You would have followed.

Rehearsing the scene a week later, Hall stirs it up: 'You're playing it as an elegy, but I have a feeling it's much hotter, tenser. Antony is "unqualitied with very shame". The lines are jagged, broken. He wants to be on his own, see no one. Cleopatra's arrival makes his sarcastic, ironic:

> Egypt, thou knewst too well
> My heart was to thy rudder tied by th'strings
> And thou shouldst tow me after.

The only hope has been to get them together – and you, Eros, Charmian and Iras, must bring that urgency on with you – but he's also dangerous, he could attack her. . . . Tony, I don't want to impose this on you, but I think he's past great feeling for her. He's like a dead man, talking of one who's alive.' (Dench: 'The greater my confidence before Actium, the more of a crash this will be. I can hardly stand up. . . .')

Now their coming together is much more loaded: a serrated uncertainty has replaced the elegaic flow. They form a long diagonal on the ground, she supplicating, he withdrawn. When he at last reclines to kiss her, the deadness in him melted by her tears, the break in tension is palpable.

Still later, when seen in the context of a run-through, more can be drawn from this scene. It had seemed to confront Antony and Cleopatra with the inescapable truth of their relationship: that she has the superior strength and that he is tied to her every move. Following their rapprochement, Hopkins instinctively pulls away and exits alone, leaving her to hurry after him. He seems to be trying to break away from her spell. . . .

This provides Judi Dench with a reason for Cleopatra's deep anxiety at the start of Scene 13: 'What shall we do, Enobarbus? . . . Is Antony or we in fault for this?' When Antony enters, the continuing tension between him and Cleopatra makes the women rush together. Hall: 'He then sets up a personal challenge to Caesar: it's his paranoia, the unbalanced "bunker mentality".' (This Hall enacts, squaring up like a prizefighter, dancing on his toes, thumbing the side of his nose.)

Growing dismay at this behaviour sharpens Cleopatra's own instincts for survival. She is disorientated and fearful of what Caesar intends. After her agonizing wait, instead of the monster she expects, the courtly Thidias arrives – and she is ready to hear his offers. To him (Des Adams) Hall says: 'You're Mr Candour, Mr Nice. Your objective – to woo and placate her on Caesar's behalf.'

THIDIAS   He knows that you embraced not Antony
           As you did love but as you feard him.

CLEOPATRA   Oh!

Into that 'Oh!', Dench puts a raft of meaning: 'Oh, what a surprise!', 'Oh, that's an angle to try . . .', 'Oh, does he really believe that?', cautious 'Oh', calculated 'Oh', affectedly meek 'Oh', cynical 'Oh'. Her artful ambiguity continues:

> He is a god and knows
> What is most right. Mine honour was not yielded
> But conquered merely.

And such is Cleopatra's inconsistency that, as Hall says, 'The audience should be terribly unsure about what game she is playing: is she being disloyal to Antony, or playing for time for both their sakes?' (This is the epitome of Hall's 'you shouldn't ever let them get a single idea of her'.)

(Nor, from Dench's point of view, is there a single answer. Cleopatra *would* be ambivalent. Thidias' attitude throws her. She can never resist a seductive overture, *and* she knows that it is politically advisable to negotiate, *and* Antony has been awful to her. So all these feelings would be operating. . . . Afterwards, of course, she would rationalize her behaviour to Antony – 'I was only doing it for you, dear' – and believe it to be the truth.)

Enobarbus has no doubts. Sure that Cleopatra is succumbing to Thidias' sweet-talk, he goes to fetch his master: 'Sir, sir, thou art so leaky/[that] Thy dearest quit thee.' Antony enters as Thidias is kissing Cleopatra's hand and interprets it as pure betrayal.

Hall: 'He misreads her fear of Caesar for coldness towards himself. This is a key scene. His defeat at Actium has destroyed his self-confidence.' Having had Thidias dragged away to be flogged, he directs a stream of verbal brutality at Cleopatra:

> You were half blasted ere I knew you. Ha!

> You have been a boggler ever

and

> I found you as a morsel cold upon
> Dead Caesar's trencher. Nay you were a fragment
> Of Gnaeus Pompey's. . . .

Now all Cleopatra/Dench's emotional resources go into winning back his trust. At the end of the scene she drops to her knees, hanging on to Antony (with tears in her eyes) as she confirms her love. When he is finally convinced, his courage seems renewed:

> I will be treble-sinewed, hearted, breathed
> And fight maliciously. . . .

> . . . . Come on my queen,
> There's sap in't yet! The next time I do fight,
> I'll make death love me for I will contend
> Even with his pestilent scythe.

But it is a hollow show, as Enobarbus well knows: having lost his
judgement and only sustained by the ghost of his courage, Antony is
now completely vulnerable and at risk.

Before the next run-through Judi Dench decides to 'jump around
more'. Once it starts, Hopkins pushes Antony's destructive drunkenness as far as it will go. It renders him dangerously unaware of
Caesar's potential in Part One of the play, so that he treats him more
like a bothersome puppy than a serious contender for world power.
In Part Two, defeat has him roving round, dazed, stumbling, crying
(literally) with self-pity. His inebriation helps to dull the pain, gives
added licence to his fits of rage (he upturns a goblet of wine over
Thidias). Afterwards, Dench is full of questions: how would
Cleopatra position herself in relation to Antony's collapse? As Hall
has said, although she has won him back from Rome, the relationship is not what it was – and keeps breaking down; the strain between
them is beginning to haunt every scene. . . .

When Antony comes upon Cleopatra holding out her hand for
Thidias to kiss, for instance, he smiles genially. Somewhat nerv-
ously, she smiles back and goes to embrace him, only to be roughly
pushed aside as he turns ugly:

> Favours, by Jove that thunders!

To repay her for the pain she has caused him, it is with a bitter
sarcasm that he reminds her of Octavia:

> Have I my pillow left unpressed in Rome,
> Foreborne the getting of a lawful race
> And by a gem of women, to be abused
> By one that looks on feeders?

The very passion with which they make up seems a barometer of
neurosis: it measures the depth of the wounds that have been
inflicted.

Reacting moment to moment during the run, Dench had shown a
perplexed anxiety in Cleopatra: Antony's mood swings put a distance
between them. Miranda Foster and Helen Fitzgerald had moved

away whenever he erupted in anger, and Enobarbus' increasing alienation from his master had been manifest in Michael Bryant. The unpredictability of Hopkins/Antony had infused the scenes with dramatic tension. Where each actor had instinctively modulated their own performance round him, they will now have to consolidate their responses.

A week later, Dench is still grappling with the through-line of her character in Part Two. Her uncertainty surfaces in a query about the 'choreography' of Act III Scene 13 – that same Thidias scene. During Antony's tirade against the man, 'We three girls feel spread out like ducks across a wall. . . .'

The director suggests that Charmian and Iras take refuge stage left, whilst Cleopatra crosses from centre stage to stand quietly in front of them. Once Thidias is dragged away after being whipped, she steps forward to confront Antony: 'Have you done yet?'

Hall: 'We should hate Cleopatra for seeming to sell Antony down the river, and then we should hate Antony for his grotesque, irresponsible behaviour. Judi, you're well aware that this treatment of Caesar's ambassador is political disaster. . . . She's like a rock in the middle of all his fury and cuts him down to size, this maudlin, vulnerable man who has failed. So hang on to that implacable calm. Refuse to indulge his self-pity:

> Alack our terrene moon
> Is now eclipsed and it portends alone
> The fall of Antony.

'He's saying "You see, it's all over. There's nothing left but my end", to which her answer is, "Fine, I'll wait around to watch that", "I must stay his time". It's only when he questions her feeling for him ("Cold-hearted towards me?") that the tears that she has been holding on to from the start of the scene, come. She makes him recover his courage, but in fact he's a broken man – and she knows it.'

Although Hall is absolutely sure about this, that Cleopatra would conceal her vulnerability until the last moment, Dench needs convincing. The path she has been following after Actium was one of overt emotionalism. Penitent and desperate to maintain the relationship, wouldn't she protest her support for Antony at the first opportunity?

'Part of the fascination of Cleopatra is her great courage and resilience,' argues the director. 'That innate knowledge of when to humble herself (as after Actium) and when to stand in the eye of the storm and refuse to accept guilt.'

(He is beginning to throw out challenges which can be unsettling. Change the attitude behind one line and it has a 'knock-on' effect: all the other cards tumble. . . And time is running out. As I see it, he is pushing the play away from romanticism towards a passionate, defining boldness: 'forget the soft options; let's dig out the conflicts and contrasts in their characters, the surprises in each scene'.)

Before Judi Dench can accept the change, she wrestles with the interpretation of 'I must stay his time': despite the 'his', Hall is convinced that she addresses Antony directly. As a key to Cleopatra's attitude to him and the steeliness in her own character, its overall effect needs to be rationalized. (She will also talk to Peggy Ashcroft about *her* handling of the emotions involved – a goodly image of one actress passing the baton to another – and gain her insight into an earlier line in the scene: in reply to Antony's taunt that she save herself by sending his grizzled head to Caesar, Cleopatra's 'That head, my lord?' should contain all her love for him.)

I perceive the way Dench works to be a careful layering process (which is in no way to exclude the intuitive leaps and on-the-spot inventiveness – but she does put down very solid foundations). It is therefore of great concern when a piece of the intricate structure is replaced. Since Anthony Hopkins tends to work in emotional 'slabs', minor adjustments are for him less painful. Hopkins: 'The all-pervading love is still there, isn't it? But it gets buried in disaster and only re-emerges at the end.'

Hall nods, thinks about it, then says: 'We end up feeling immense pity for them, both, for him in his madness, and for her, that she is entangled with it and remains staunch.'

The altered emotional path of Scene 13 turns Enobarbus' last lines into stark statements about Antony's condition. (Hall: 'This is "crazy", "sick". It's the augurer's voice, almost.') And, I would add, the psychiatrist's voice:

> Now he'll outstare the lightning. To be furious
> Is to be frighted out of fear. . . .
>
> . . . . and I see still
> A diminution in our captain's brain

Restores his heart. When valour preys on reason,
It eats the sword it fights with.

Against the mounting chaos and despair in Antony and Cleopatra's camp, Hall asks that in the interim Act III Scene 12, Caesar's entourage bring on to the stage a great confidence in their leader. He is in a supreme position to treat with Antony. The humble School-master is ridiculed, so denigrating the seriousness of his mission: clearly the war is at an end – and Caesar is going to be a ruthless and exacting victor.

(I had shown Graham Sinclair a book* in which Maecenas, Caesar's wealthy 'backer', is described as being 'a sophisticated and effete Etruscan'. He latched on to that 'effete' with delight – it is both relief and inspiration to find a peg on which to hang an underwritten part – and planned to build it into his characterization. Renaissance dress, the blue velvet cloak of Maecenas' costume, will help. . . . It will be interesting to watch this broad-shouldered, bass-voiced actor work his way into something so against type.)

Act IV Scene 2 is a pitiful parody of the 'one other gaudy night' to be shared with 'All my sad captains', which Antony had bravely called for at the end of Act III. Instead, the household servants enter in a cluster, then form a line down which he goes, shaking each by the hand and, as he speaks, grasping the last round the shoulders and leading him apart. Hopkins' gestures and tone evoke a general with his men the night before an ill-fated battle:

> I wish I could be made so many men
> And all of you clapped up together in
> An Antony, that I might do you service
> as good as you have done. . . .

That Enobarbus is moved to tears by his leader's humiliation and despair becomes wholly understandable.

The extent of Antony's decline is firmly established over the next fortnight. Halfway through the ninth week of rehearsal (Thursday 12 March), the company starts to go over Act IV Scene 2 again. Suddenly and unusually, Hall is called away to arbitrate at a crucial meeting (over proposed cutbacks in the technical departments).

---

* *Cleopatra* by Michael Grant (Weidenfeld & Nicolson, 1972).

In their director's absence, the actors go into a huddle and come up with a version of the scene which they feel follows the path of the play. It is full of energy, optimism and briskness – and makes false connections. Having picked up on Antony's hollow bravado at the end of the Thidias scene, the industrious group has lost touch with its core, his paranoia and disintegration.

Returning the next morning, Hall sets the play back on course, forging authentic links with what has been, what is to follow: 'Until we've run and run the play, I've no idea how drunk Antony is going to be in each scene. What I *do* know is that this is the lowest he sinks, the most self-indulgent and irrational. We have just found out (in Act IV Scene 1) that many of his 'noble captains' have deserted:

> CAESAR   Within our files there are,
> Of those who served Mark Antony but late,
> Enough to fetch him in.

Now Antony shocks the servants by treating them as intimates and calling on their pity. It has to be a painful spectacle.'

(Poring over the text, it suddenly dawns on me that Antony is, in fact, so doom-struck that he is hallucinating when he addresses his servants; he confuses them with those very captains he has lost:

> . . . . You have served me well
> And kings have been your fellows.

and

> Scant not my cups and make as much of me
> As when mine empire was your fellow too
> And suffered my command.

Described by Enobarbus as 'one of those odd tricks which sorrow shoots/Out of the mind', it is a perceptual distortion brought on by despair. Hall disagrees but I remain convinced, for – his teaching! – the evidence is all there in the text.)

The scene now takes on an appropriately sombre, nightmarish quality. Hopkins stumbles about, giving vent to his emotion, encircled by horrified onlookers, frozen in disbelief.

After Michael Bryant's dry: 'You helped us out of that one, Peter. Ten out of ten,' Hall recalls working on a difficult scene with Ralph

Richardson. Richardson's comment at the end had been ruminative. 'I don't like directors much. . . .'

Too often, actors are at the mercy of weak and incompetent directors, or of those who see themselves as puppet-masters. Either left to flounder or strait-jacketed, it is not surprising that they are increasingly vociferous about taking some of the power into their own hands. The Actors' Company, started by Ian McKellen and Edward Petherbridge, was an early attempt at self-direction by actors working as a team.

Most recently, Kenneth Branagh and David Parfitt started Renaissance Theatre, also actor-oriented, and got the sympathetic direction they were after, by inviting fellow-actors Judi Dench, Derek Jacobi and Geraldine McEwan to direct for them. Companies such as Joint Stock and Shared Experience, founded on actor/director/writer collaboration, ensure that everyone participates in creative responsibility and control – often with thrilling results.

Yet, whatever the company structure, a production ultimately needs a strong, centralized vision. Without Hall, the actors involved in the episode above had gone off at a tangent, regardless of combined quality, creativity and experience. It was brutal confirmation that someone must carry the overview of a play, and guide it continuously towards clarification of this view.

Demonstrably, definition of one scene has an impact on those which build off it. Because Cleopatra's imperious stance prior to Actium had been forcibly scored, the underlying currents in Act IV Scene 4 rise to the surface. As Hall points out, this later scene is an attempt to blot out the disaster, when she behaved like a man and took part in the battle. This time as Antony prepares for war, she buckles on his armour with a deliberate 'feminine' ineptitude and he makes her into 'the little woman', left behind when the men go off to fight:

> O love,
> That thou couldst see my wars today and knew'st
> The royal occupation;

Hopkins has started to work in boots and a metal breastplate which goes over his head and is buckled either side, turning him into a stocky St George.

To the soldiers who escort Antony off, Hall says: 'You're a small band, in danger of being wiped out. The only hope for your lives is to build up his confidence and determination' (a confidence painfully dented in the next scene when he learns of Enobarbus' desertion).

At a later stage, following the line being established in Part Two of the play – Antony's frailty in the face of defeat and Cleopatra's resilience – this scene begins to have the feel of a charade. With her support, Antony has pulled himself together and is joking and optimistic whilst she, the pragmatist, has to conceal her fears. It is quite a shift for Dench: we must sense the tears beneath her apparent high spirits.

Afterwards, she sits making notes: 'I've never scribbled on a script so much. Things are changing. . . . I'm beginning to know what to hang Cleopatra on for the whole middle section of the play. It's better, isn't it?' She sounds buoyant.

The second battle is restaged, with Agrippa and his soldiers running on to the stage from one aisle of the auditorium and exiting up the opposite aisle, in flight from Antony's men.

Hall decides to break away from formality in Act IV Scene 8, and have the small, unexpectedly victorious army come down the centre aisle in joyful disarray. He asks the actors to react freely; whooping and cheering they spread themselves across the stage, sheathing swords, embracing, removing helmets, swigging from flasks, throwing themselves to the ground, visibly shedding the tensions of battle. The scene starts with a flood of energy. To alert Cleopatra, Antony bangs on the doors upstage.

Emerging, Dench conveys her wonder and disbelief at the triumph. (Hall: 'The problem with this scene is that it's so easy to be conventional.' Dench: 'And get settled. . . .') At first she would react cautiously, there would be tension between her and Antony. To Hopkins, Hall says: 'You have to go from the spellbinding to the erotic – it's very sexy writing. We're in an enchanted "something" until it breaks back to the normal world with "What girl!"

'Scarus, lying wounded and blood-soaked between you, is the emblem of victory and escape from death, of courage and nobility. He's the young warrior that Antony used to be, the emblem that brings them together, physically.'

When Antony tells Cleopatra to offer her hand to Scarus – 'Kiss it, my warrior' – we are made very conscious of the parallel situation (when Thidias' kiss aroused Antony to fury): he is making amends.

Hall now feels very strongly that Hopkins and Dench should *not* touch until the end, so that tension is maintained.

There is general agreement to set the scene in the early evening: Cleopatra will come through the doors with the light behind her, two flambeaux illuminating the darkened stage. Dench, only half joking: 'Oh, it would be wonderful to play it all in the dark, back to the audience, way upstage!'

At moments like this one gets a glimpse of her anxiety about a part which is notoriously difficult. Both she and Hopkins have spoken of waking at four in the morning, with the lines running through their heads. Once she talked of a feeling of despair . . . another time asked 'Am I too English?' Hopkins' anxieties focus, overtly, on his difficulties with 'these tongue-twisting lines'. For all his apparent freedom and lack of self-consciousness, he is later to say: 'I have to make a tremendous effort to let myself go – to rely on my instincts and all the work laid in at rehearsals – before I can start to enjoy a part and liberate its elements.' He would like less of what Hall had called his 'dark, Welsh side': 'Too much introspection doesn't help, does it?' Continually forcing himself through boundaries, he quotes from Goethe along the lines of 'Be bold and your courage will conquer the darkness'.

When asked (at the end of the rehearsal period) what aspect of Antony's character he finds most difficult, the actor says unhesitatingly: 'His glamour and attractiveness'. Often cast in films and television series for his romantic appeal, Hopkins has a very different self-image: 'I mean, look at me. Short, grey-haired. . . . I find it very difficult to go out onstage and lean against the furniture with, you know, the right kind of confidence. It feels ridiculous. Then I think, what the hell, I'll believe I'm like that. . . .' (In an industry which deals in idealized images, writer David Thomson describes the first meeting between Jack Nicholson and Warren Beatty:* Nicholson approaches, looks up at Beatty who is five or six inches taller than he is, whistles and says: 'Now *that's* what a film star's supposed to look like.')

Judi Dench, too, finds most difficult about her character the need to fight physical preconceptions. In her case they are not so much personal as those of an audience who expect to see a Cleopatra who is

* *Warren Beatty – A Life & A Story*, by David Thomson (Secker & Warburg, 1987).

dark, slim and young – what Peter Hall called the 'Cecil B. De Mille, G. B. Shaw, Liz Taylor undulating-sexpot image'. 'But,' says Dench, 'the more we go on, the more I am convinced that Peter has got it right, the play is about middle-aged people.'

In both of them there is great vulnerability: the larger the role, the greater the reputation of the actress or actor involved, the more they risk in exposure.

There is a sharply effective moment in Act IV Scene 6, whilst Caesar is preparing for the second battle. As Tim Pigott-Smith commands:

> Plant those that have revolted in the van
> That Antony may seem to spend his fury
> Upon himself.

he looks with deep contempt at Michael Bryant, standing awkwardly in the background, and Bryant seems to shrink into himself with pain and humiliation, feelings compounded by hearing of Antony's generosity towards him. 'I am alone the villain of the earth . . ./This blows my heart,' says Enobarbus.

Bryant builds on this emotion for his death scene. To avoid the elegaic, Hall drops in the suggestion that he show more signs of fever. Having created a fully-rounded character almost from the first, Bryant is now so rooted in it that I am finding it difficult to separate the actor from the part he plays. As, in Enobarbus, powerful emotion is concealed behind a bluff manner, only to show through at the end, Bryant is uncovering, inch by inch, the grief which finally kills him: its outward manifestations are jerky, arrested movements and irregular speech rhythms.

By Act IV Scene 12, Antony's brave veneer has gone. Hall: 'I think his spirit is broken. He's a hunted man. And this time it is not his drinking nor Enobarbus' desertion, but the fact that the enemy is determined to fight at sea, symbol of disaster for him since Actium. Since he is afraid of it, and has sent others to do his fighting for him (in the third battle), he's ashamed to look Scarus in the eye. It is the final humiliation of the man of honour. Once upon a time he would have told someone to shin up a tree and see what's happening. Now he goes himself – "Where yond pine does stand/I shall discover all. I'll bring thee word . . ." – and it is pathetic.'

When Antony sees his fleet surrender to Caesar's, he suffers complete disillusionment. The strain in the relationship between him and Cleopatra comes to a head – as does his paranoia. 'He is going to pieces physically,' senses Hall: 'Tony, I believe he gets the shakes on "The shirt of Nessus is upon me". . . . '

The director points out the rich mix of metaphors in Antony's soliloquy of loss:

> The hearts
> That spanieled me at heels. . . .
> . . . . do discandy, melt their sweets
> On blossoming Caesar and this pine is barked
> That overtopped them all.

'Trust your middle register,' he advises Hopkins. 'It will grow if you don't resort to the strident.'

On the Friday morning of the ninth week, they get to grips with the action of Act IV Scene 14 (Eros' death and Antony's attempted suicide). Malcolm Ranson is in attendance.

Jerry Flynn works intently, almost covertly. His is a slow gestation period: one observes him responding to fellow-actors, taking direction, making connections and offering useful suggestions, but reining in his characterization, presumably until he has integrated all its facets. The process is almost imperceptible: I am intrigued to see it come to fruition. . . . Meanwhile, he rapidly absorbs Ranson's instructions for falling on his sword: the weapon, in fact, goes under the arm furthest from the audience, whilst Flynn collapses over it, concealing his sleight of hand. Following this, Antony Hopkins pushes his sword in towards his stomach whilst facing the audience full on. 'The effect becomes convincing if you dramatize the intent,' is Ranson's advice: so the thrust is made bold and the hilt of the sword is moved violently from side to side as Hopkins crumples to his knees and speaks through gasps of pain.

Wanting to understand the logistics of the sequence, and its problems or further possibilities, Hall tries this himself: 'What we must avoid is "end is nigh" nobility. It must be a scramble, full of panic and confusion. I like the idea of Eros dying centre-stage, Antony off-centre.'

Hall had talked to Hopkins of Antony's sense of approaching death. Again, he personalizes the emotions involved: 'You know that feeling – why is it me in this nightmare and not someone else? He moves between illusion and reality. His whole life has come to nothing. The line – "Whose heart I thought I had, for she had mine" – must contain all your love for Cleopatra.'

Iain Ormsby-Knox (Mardian) comes in to report Cleopatra's supposed death, using a falsetto voice for the first time. When Hopkins starts:

I will o'ertake thee Cleopatra . . .

Hall asks him to *explain* the rest to us: just this word elicits a moving simplicity. 'Antony is resigned. He sees the futility of life and looks towards another ghostly plane "Where souls do couch on flowers". His call to "Eros!" is, of course, also a call to the god of love,' adds Hall.

There is real tension while Antony waits for the sword blow from Eros, horror when Eros turns it on himself and dies instantly. By contrast, Antony's inability to achieve the same clean end and his desperate cries for someone to finish him off, turn a heroic gesture into one which is wretched. It is a disturbing revelation.

Hall orchestrates the responses to these cries so that the members of the Guard pick up on Hopkins' tone, now soft:

ANTONY   O make an end
       Of what I have begun.
2ND GUARD   The star is fallen.
1ST GUARD   And time is at his period.
ALL GUARDS   Alas and woe!

– now loud, with the pentameter filled as they rush away in different directions:

ANTONY   Let him that loves me strike me dead.
1ST GUARD   Not I.
2ND GUARD   Nor I.
3RD GUARD   Nor anyone.

Increasingly, the director is going for a choral effect in group responses, coaching the actors to beat the lines – and pauses – internally.

After Decretas, vulture-like, has grabbed Antony's discarded sword (which 'shown to Caesar, with this tidings,/Shall enter me with him'), Diomedes comes on to discover the dying Antony. As

Bob Arnold, in this cameo role, kneels behind Antony, supporting his shoulders and keening with grief, he brings an authentic note of horror and compassion to the scene. Hopkins gives a broken laugh when he hears that Cleopatra's reported death was just another of her wiles; he seems to be laughing at himself and the irony of his destiny – there is not a word of bitterness against her.

Ranson demonstrates how to lift and carry off the body of Eros: standing astride Jerry Flynn's legs, he pulls him up to a sitting position by his arms, then leans forward, and in one quick movement lifts the whole body over his shoulder. Carefully supervised, the actors try it.

Another substitute monument is wheeled forward: six feet high, made up of several layered platforms, it has a balustrade across half the top. The rest is exposed so that Antony can later be seen, cradled in Cleopatra's arms.

Dench had wanted to know why Cleopatra sent word to Antony that she had killed herself: was it fear or attention-seeking? Hall: 'It's fear that drives her to the monument, then she wants to punish Antony for threatening her.' Now, at the start of Act IV Scene 15, she has a premonition of the finality of it all and almost anticipates Antony's death:

O Charmian, I will never go from hence.

When he is carried in, Hall feels he should be a mess, blood and guts hanging out: 'His desire for one last kiss is a parody of *Romeo and Juliet*. The women winching him aloft should be desperate and clumsy.'

At each stage of Antony's dying, the director is stressing the anti-heroic in order to set up the paradox: Antony, the great hero in the world's eyes, botches his own suicide, whilst Cleopatra, the so-called strumpet, will die in state, with a noble dignity. It is a skilful way of tackling an obvious problem: Cleopatra's death can be anti-climactic, coming as it does a whole act after Antony's. By undercutting the latter, giving it a frail human dimension, the drama is left with a further plateau to which to climb. When Antony does die, Cleopatra is enraged: it is anarchy, the apocalypse:

The crown o'th'earth doth melt. . . .

Again, the note is not elegaic but more of a protest. She swoons and seems dead. Once revived, her mind is made up: she is resolved to end her own life as quickly as possible.

Now the action switches to Caesar's camp. The beginning of Act V is redone, to give it extra pace and excitement: Caesar enters with his entourage, telling Dolabella to go and persuade Antony to yield. Suddenly Decretas appears, brandishing Antony's sword. Caesar calls out and soldiers rush on to defend him, their swords at the ready.

Caesar's response to Decretas' news is a paean of regret for the man who dominated their lives. Emotion drives him to hyperbole:

> The breaking of so great a thing should make
> A greater crack.

and he has to fight back his tears:

> . . . it is tidings
> To wash the eyes of kings.

Tim Pigott-Smith: 'It is a scene about the inadequacy of what he is saying. . . .' We get the public statement about all that Antony embodied:

> . . . in the name lay
> A moiety of the world

and the courage with which he died: it contrasts discomfortingly with the tawdry reality we have just witnessed.

Pigott-Smith has a difficult set of emotions to reconcile: in Part Two of the play, his Caesar has grown in confidence and smugness in the face of Antony's decline. Now he has to make credible his admiration and, indeed, love for the man he harshly dismissed as 'the old ruffian'. He does this by returning to the idolization he explored at the beginning of the play. (As I watch, I wonder how much of Caesar's emotion is for public consumption? This would be behaviour appropriate to the occasion and, of course, now that Antony no longer threatens his lust for supremacy, he can afford to be moved.)

> We could not stall together
> In the whole world. But yet let me lament
> With tears as sovereign as the blood of hearts
> That thou, my brother, my competitor

In top of all design, my mate in empire,
Friend and companion in the front of war,
The arm of mine own body and the heart
Where mine his thoughts did kindle – that our stars,
Unreconciliable, should divide
Our equalness to this.

At the entry of the Egyptian, pure self-interest returns. How can Caesar stop Cleopatra killing herself so that he can display her upon his triumphal return to Rome? (And this a moment after he has protested his honourable and kindly intentions – 'For Caesar cannot live/To be ungentle' – a line for which the actor sinks to one knee, the better to convince the cringing Egyptian messenger of his sincerity.) Operating with total clarity, some of his men efficiently deployed to fulfil his plans, he at once turns to the others with fake integrity: '. . . see/How hardly I was drawn into this war'. He has become a consummate politician.

As usual, Tim Pigott-Smith works with immense care and sensitivity. His scenes can take time, until he feels comfortable with a change in emotional gear or an interaction with a fellow-actor. The process is meticulous.

Act V Scene 2. That Cleopatra seems to have come to terms with Antony's death should come as a bit of a shock, feels Hall:

My desolation does begin to make
A better life.

The button of tension is her resolve to kill herself, set against Caesar's determination that she be taken alive. Dench starts the scene very contained, until the obscenity of her capture, when she tries to kill herself with her own dagger. At Dolabella's arrival, she turns inwards, with a terrible despair. (Andrew Wadsworth, with his shaggy hair and moustache, always in boots and duffle-coat, is a calm, reassuring presence.)

Once again, Peter Hall proscribes the conventional elegiac which, given the poetic imagery and language, would be easy to slip into: 'Judi, the "I dreamt there was an emperor Antony . . ." stuff is concrete. She's recalling him, finding the words. So be specific. . . .'

                    . . . . For his bounty,
There was no winter in't; an Antony it was
That grew the more by reaping. His delights

> Were dolphin-like; they showed his back above
> The element they lived in.   In his livery
> Walked crowns and crownets. . . .

At once the colouring of the lines becomes more vivid.

Dolabella, the ladies' man, has been sent to keep Cleopatra talking, but is seduced into disclosing Caesar's plans: he is Cleopatra's last lover, agree Dench and Hall. His gentleness and courtesy (he calls her 'most noble empress') contrast poignantly with the scene's preceding brutality.

Where is Seleucus/Dan Thorndike to come from? Hall: 'On the Elizabethan stage, the whole space would be the monument. You'd call and he'd be there. . . .' Dench: 'But we've set up so potently that Cleopatra locked herself into the monument with just her closest followers. . . .' They restage the scene using the aisles through the auditorium: Dolabella comes down on to the stage from the right, Caesar, centre, and Seleucus from the left. Charmian hands Cleopatra an account-book (and Emma Lloyd makes a note of the great gilded tome required from the props department). Hall: 'The wealth of Egypt was enough to unbalance the finances of the whole Roman Empire.' For what Malcolm Ranson calls 'duffing up Dan' – Cleopatra's attack on Seleucus – he shows Dench how to go for his eyes with a dramatic but arrested gesture, and Thorndike how to fall backwards in a series of controlled moves. At Caesar's exit, Dench hurls the book from her violently: her wealth has lost its bargaining power.

> . . . I am again for Cydnus
> To meet Mark Antony

is regular, weighty. The tone becomes colloquial when the Guardsman (Mike Hayward again) brings notice of the Clown, hesitant about letting in such a 'rural fellow'.

'He brings me liberty', says Cleopatra, when left alone:

> My resolution's placed and I have nothing
> Of woman in me. Now from head to foot
> I am marble-constant; now the fleeting moon
> No planet is of mine.

Peter Hall makes it clear that, although commentators say that Cleopatra is the only great Shakespearean character without a soliloquy, they are wrong – for this is it, a key exposure of herself to the audience.

To John Bluthal: 'Be warmer, shrewder. He's a kindly messenger of death, full of compassion for a woman taking her life. Observe the punctuation more. The prose breaks against the verse.' Since this is Cleopatra's farewell to everything, including Egypt (which the Clown, as the 'salt of the earth', represents), Hall feels that the scene should have a protracted quality. But she is also 'a woman on the brink of jumping out of the window': beneath Judi Dench's calm acceptance is an undercurrent of vast sadness and regret.

Finally, the mood in which she is prepared for death by Charmian and Iras is of desire wanting to be satisfied – excited, anticipatory and blissful.

Using a frisky North American garter snake, (which has supplanted the black racer) the mechanics of the end of the play are worked out: at which point Dench is to take up the asps (one live, the second, a realistic prop), when Miranda Foster is to take one from her and then conceal it from the Guard. All fiddly stuff. Cleopatra is seated in front of the monument, Charmian and Iras fall to the floor on either side as they die. Caesar/Pigott-Smith re-enters down the centre aisle with his entourage. Hall is planning that Cleopatra, when dead, be carried through the auditorium on her throne so that the last image is of Caesar watching from downstage as the procession moves up the aisle. The ceremony should give a chill sense of balance and order restored.

By examining the precise feelings revealed in each of Cleopatra's speeches after the death of Antony, her emotional journey from raging self-pity to ultimate ecstasy has been given texture and humanity: one is dragged through the pain to a kind of catharsis.

It was while they were tracing this journey, that Judi Dench asked me whether there was any tradition of suicide amongst the Ptolemies. When I told her that, on the evidence, they would sacrifice anyone, including parents and children, to hang on to life and power, she was delighted: 'Although Peter says that after Antony dies, the audience are longing for Cleopatra to join him, I keep finding moments when she seems to want to live.' It is not coincidental that she is essentially a realist, whilst Hall is a self-confessed romantic; difference in outlook influences interpretation of the text.

There is a paradox, expressed in the writing: 'It is Cleopatra's unique love for Antony,' says Peter Hall, 'which makes her aware of the futility of life without him (". . . there is nothing left remarkable/ Beneath the visiting moon") and the triumph in rising above earthly matters:

> 'Tis paltry to be Caesar:
> Not being Fortune, he's but Fortune's knave,
> . . . And it is great
> To do that thing that ends all other deeds. . . .

'But it is her instinct as a survivor which keeps her politicking until the end, not least to ensure the future of her dynasty.' His explanation leaves room for both approaches.

CHAPTER 8
Going on Elsewhere

In the rehearsal room the cast is immured from tensions in the wider organization, except when the axe falls directly: at the beginning of March they greet with dismay the news that *Antony and Cleopatra* is now unlikely to visit Greece and Egypt. A revised touring agreement with the technicians' union, BETA, has not yet been reached, and the National has already had to cancel twenty-five weeks of touring with a cross-section of productions, in Britain and abroad.

This is part of a larger dispute which has been dragging on between technicians and management for over a year. The 1985 Rayner Report, commissioned by the National to review its own efficiency, recommended various cost-saving measures. By closing the metal, armoury and carpentry workshops (and putting the work of these and of the NT cleaning services out to private contractors), and by changing entrenched working practices backstage (such as the separation of props and scene shifting), a technical staff of 350 could be reduced by between 60 and 70. The estimated saving of not less than £600,000 over three years would help to offset the drastic cuts in Arts Council subsidy to the National (£1.1 million in two years) – cuts that have so far fallen mainly on productions themselves, which are cheaper and fewer.

These proposals are being hotly contested by the technicians – their union calls them 'a narrow-minded exercise in theatrical butchery': apart from the obvious redundancies, as an increasing amount of construction work is done outside the theatre, quality and timing become more difficult to control. The metal workshop and armoury are being wound down as *Antony and Cleopatra* rehearses, and stage management are feeling the effects of the reduced support.

As the National's overall artistic director, Peter Hall is, of course, in the thick of the negotiations. To an extent he has precipitated them, by opting for confrontation: 'I want this to be my gift to my successor, Richard Eyre. He should not inherit problems and working practices that stretch back through the ages.'* But except on one occasion when he was called away to a meeting in connection with the conflict (and the actors continued on their own – above, p. 81), he does not allow his managerial concerns to interfere with rehearsals.

In the construction and other departments, too, progress continues, seemingly unimpeded: any resentment towards management is outweighed by regard for the next production.

In the paintshop, the vast backcloth, 11.9 metres high by 30 metres wide, hangs from a frame. Over a coating of Idendum (which renders the canvas fireproof but leaves it flexible) colour is being built up in layers. At this stage it is covered with red and gold swirls, as is the circular floor, constructed in the NT carpenters' shop and laid out in panels. Temporary wooden inserts fill the tracks for the movable doors and walls. Later, as cyclorama and floor near completion, Alison Chitty will describe them as 'a giant red coughdrop'.

By the sixth week of rehearsal, she had resolved most of the practical and constructional details of the set. The walls will be winched back and forth from behind the cyclorama, the central door-section by a man seated within it. This section, a feat of engineering, will open out to form the monument. A concealed ladder will provide access to the balcony on top, whilst, below, a double set of gates will be pulled out when the doors are folded back. Kemps, an outside firm, are making the doors, Terry Murphy's company, the walls.

In the Props Department, banners are under construction, some with wreaths, others with Roman insignia. One is tested for weight during a rehearsal: it features a crested helmet above a bronzed centurion's tunic, with a swathe of blue silk falling to the base of the pole. There are heavy coils of rope to make up the rigging for Pompey's galley. Yolande Jeffrey, Head Property Buyer, has just been asked for ship's lanterns for this scene, and luggage for Antony and Octavia's departure (for which Chitty must now submit details

---

* This was a gift he would be able to make. On 4 November 1987 what he called 'a breakthrough agreement' was arrived at, introducing more flexible working practices, consolidating overtime payments into a new basic wage – and resolving the touring issues (too late, alas, for *Antony and Cleopatra* to benefit).

Antony on the shoulders of Mardian (Iain Ormsby-Knox)
— the procession with which the play opens.   *Act I Scene 1*

Charmian (Miranda Foster) and Cleopatra
CLEOPATRA: O happy horse, to bear the weight of Antony.   *Act I Scene 5*

Caesar and Lepidus await Antony's return to Rome
CAESAR: Let his shames quickly/Drive him to Rome.   *Act I Scene 4*

Cleopatra attacks the Messenger (Jerry Flynn)
who has brought news of Antony's marriage to Octavia.   *Act II Sc*

Pompey with the pirate, Menas.

The feast on Pompey's galley — with rope rigging.
Menas in foreground.   *Act II Scene 7*

Octavia torn between her brother and her husband, whilst Lepidus looks on.
Antony and Octavia depart for Athens.   *Act III Scene 2*

Antony and Cleopatra form a long diagonal.
Charmian looks on.   *Act III Scene 11*

ANTONY: You were half blasted ere I knew you. Ha!   *Act III Scene 13*

Reconciliation (below left).   *Act III Scene 13*

ENOBARBUS: O sovereign mistress of true melancholy,
The poisonous damp of night dispose upon me . . .
A master-leaver and a fugitive.   *Act IV Scene 9*

Soldiers on sentry duty at night hear 'music i'th'air. Under the earth.'
Act IV Scene 3

Antony returns after unexpected victory in the second battle.   *Act IV Scene 8*

The dying Antony is hauled up to the monument.   *Act IV Scene 15*

CLEOPATRA: Come, thou mortal wretch
With thy sharp teeth this knot intrinsicate
Of life at once untie . . .   *Act V Scene 2*

and designs). In the carpentry workshop, wooden legs are being turned and grooved for the funeral bier in the Parthian scene.

During rehearsals, Emma Lloyd mass-produces documents for the play, cutting up pages of parchment onto which she traces maps of the Mediterranean, circa 40 BC.

Richard Pocock, Head of Props, Paintframe and Armoury, is in at a discussion with Chitty, Lloyd and Malcolm Ranson about the weaponry in the play: Lloyd assembles everything available – swords recycled from *Coriolanus*, sundry pikes and halberds. More can be borrowed from the Opera House or the RSC. Retractable swords, with which Antony and Eros can stab themselves, are being considered.

Most of the costumes are being made in the NT's Wardrobe on the fifth floor. Supervisors Stephanie Baird and Anne Watkins have received over sixty designs from Alison Chitty: Roman battledress is a classical/Renaissance fusion – sculpted leather breastplates, leg and arm greaves and draped cloaks are worn over doublets, breeches and boots. In the Alexandrian scenes, it will look as if Antony has been down to the market-place and adorned himself in an Arabic robe. Fabric colour is dark and rich for the Romans, light-filled for the Egyptians. Cleopatra and her women wear waisted full-skirted dresses over filmy underskirts. There is a North African influence in caftan outlines, baggy gathered pants for the eunuchs, turban headdresses, tassels and patterned borders.

Ready for use are bales of silk and velvet, embroidered and brocaded Indian cloth, soft calfskin for the armour, rolls of sequined braid, multi-coloured bracelets and beads, and gilded armlets. Detailed measurements have been taken for actors not already on file. Almost finished, Sally Dexter's Octavia costume, with its laced bodice and full, trailing skirt of grey raw silk, gleams from a dressmaker's dummy. Draped on another is the dazzling gold-pleated robe for Judi Dench's final scene. In the tailoring area, quilted velvet is cut at long tables, doublets are pinned and pressed.

Shoes and boots are being made by the firm of Anello and Davide. Other specialist work has been farmed out to Stephen Gregory (armour), Jenny Adey (hats) and Jean Gates (jewellery and Cleopatra's crown). Gregory has taken torso casts of the leading 'Romans' from which to mould their leather tunics.

In the NT's Wig Department, wigs for the women, and the men's hairpieces, moustaches and beards are being crafted by Joyce Beagarie and her team.

Actors start going off for fittings which Angie Bissett co-ordinates with the rehearsal schedule and lists on the daily call sheet. Alison Chitty and four members of wardrobe are present as Dan Thorndike tries on his Seleucus costume: an open, sleeveless maroon coat goes over a long, beige rough-textured robe, tied with a soft brown and beige sash. There is fine detailing in the cut. Chitty adjusts the shoulders to alter folds, and draws an outline on the fabric for the plaicing of braid. A pair of Indian slippers is selected from a large pile and there is a careful check as to whether the actor will be able to climb the ramp to the stage, kneel, fall and rise.

With over a hundred costumes to make, many of great complexity, concentration is intense. Yet the prevailing atmosphere is of order and calm.

Up in the Press Office, too, steady progress has been made. The lay-out for the programme is finalized, text and illustrations assembled. I've enjoyed being consulted about its content along the way: it has given me a function on the production beyond that of observer. All that remains is for the actors to check and, if necessary, amend their potted biographies, copies of which are distributed. John Haynes' rehearsal photographs will go into the first run of programmes, to be replaced by production shots, with actors in costume and make-up, at the time of reprinting.

On a Monday morning Paul Arditti takes everyone outside to record an assortment of group cheers including those at the rally for Pompey, those heralding the victory at Parthia, and, when Antony's fleet go over to the enemy, the mighty hail to 'Caesar!' The actors stand in the wind, overlooking the river; the noise brings people to the windows of the IBM building behind them.

Alan Cohen has started to direct understudy rehearsals and the actors switch between their 'primary' roles with Hall and the parts they are covering in the rehearsal room next door. Malcolm Ranson drills groups of soldiers, passing on skills about the wielding and wearing of swords (for higher orders they're worn on the left, lower orders unsheath them on the right since the shields they carry block the other side). There are several vigorous drum-coaching sessions in one of the sound studios and Julia Wilson-Dixon continues to do vocal sessions with individual actors wherever she can find an empty room.

Commercial sponsorship was first sought by the National for peripheral events only, the argument being that the government had built the NT and therefore had a responsibility to fund its basic work. However, the growing inadequacy of public funding had forced the theatre to seek financial support from the private sector for its mainhouse productions. Thus, Development Manager Josette Nicholls had been looking for a sponsor for *Antony and Cleopatra*.

In return she would offer due acknowledgement in all related publicity (advertisements, programmes, posters, booking leaflets and the Ceefax news roster on the front of the building itself – visible to everyone crossing Waterloo Bridge). Entertainment facilities would be made available in the theatre, where the sponsors and their guests would have a chance to meet the cast and production staff of the play. From an association with the NT, the sponsor would benefit in terms of publicity and public relations.

Nicholls, a blend of charm, tenacity and diplomacy, keeps updated files of contacts, amongst them the Ladbroke Group, which operates hotels, casinos and betting-shops, and with whom she had first been in touch in 1984. A re-approach in 1986 gave them 'first refusal' on *Antony and Cleopatra* and was endorsed by two members of the NT's active Board and fund-raising Council, Sir Peter Parker and Lois Sieff. In late February 1987, Ladbrokes made a lump-sum commitment towards the cost of the production – and Nicholls breathed an eleventh-hour sigh of relief.

CHAPTER 9
Hallstyle

By now, having sat through rehearsals day after day, I find it impossible to remain detached, not to be caught up in the working process (haunted by it, even, lines in the play, the 'tune' of certain speeches, visual images, waking me in the early hours of the morning). Having borne witness to hours of meticulous labour, how can I help but share the elation and relief when a characterization suddenly comes into focus, when a problem scene is finally 'cracked', its content laid bare in the most theatrically satisfying way? A solution may have been sought via logic and reason, but the test of its acceptability is always instinctive: it *feels* right – and that both to players and onlookers, myself amongst them.

Considered in the context of so-called 'actors' theatre' or 'directors' theatre', this is unquestionably 'playwrights' theatre' where, as far as is imaginatively possible, the writer's interior vision is being investigated and responded to. Although collaborative input has fleshed out that vision in a way which is distinctive, the inspirational core has been the text itself, first and last. Were intention and integrity in rehearsal to be assessed, I would here declare service being superlatively rendered.

However, the completed meal is yet to be served, to a paying and impartial audience. What will their instinctive reaction be? Will the route taken by Hall and his creative team resonate with them?

The play itself, despite the glamorous aura surrounding its central figures, is not an easy one. It runs almost four hours, covers vast leaps in place and time and has, throughout, language which is dense in imagery and historical detail. There is no let-up.

In this particular production, a mature director has taken on a predominantly mature cast, to embark upon a journey which makes heavy technical and emotional demands of them, and does not indulge an audience. From the start, Cleopatra and Antony are shown as excessive, arrogant, provocative. In the choice of a single, abstract set, with very few trappings, Hall has elected to rely on the writing and the ability of his actors to deliver its wealth. Nor has lush language been allowed to lapse into the soothingly elegaic or purely lyrical: whenever that threatened, the structure beneath the music, what it revealed about feeling and thought, has been reappraised and conventional delivery often stood on its head. Scene follows scene almost relentlessly. Action and words are delivered out front and, with little to blur the edges or distract, one is made to listen and absorb: 'theatre of confrontation', it could be called. Such a rigorous method of presentation takes courage. It certainly takes a director with full confidence in his playwright and his players.

The pattern of rehearsals has a detectable rhythm:

> work on scene-scene-scene-run-through
> work on scene-scene-scene-run-through

When scenes are done in isolation the pace is thoughtful, careful, unhurried: a dialogue goes on between director and cast before, during, after. A run-through is, by contrast, a quasi-performance; Hall stands back as actors and stage management take the reins.

After it is over, he is back at the helm, giving notes. A run in the sixth week elicited a general comment about the verse-speaking: 'It's all a little stiff, the way you phrase is still somewhat self-conscious. No character uses the antitheses without awareness; so find them – and the alliterations and rhymes – then make them your own. To reiterate an old saw: a lot of you still throw yourselves by breathing in the wrong place and, projecting in the Olivier, you'll feel it even more. The rule is, mark the end of the line with a breath, if you need one, and then breathe at the mid-line, if there is a full stop.'

Often the flow of the play illuminates specifics of character: one particular run-through made Hall aware of the sexual bitterness in Pompey's references to Antony and Cleopatra: 'His sense of virtue is manic, John Knoxian, Paisleyan. He's an obsessed demi-god, bent on revenging his father and bringing in a new puritanism. Obsessiveness – and his low flashpoint – is the key to him and makes him a real threat to power in the Roman world.' (This not only affects the way in which Schofield handles his lines – his movement becomes panther-like and lethal.)

Again, clued by the text – 'The language is almost distraught' – Hall feels that Caesar's reaction to Antony's death is also expressive of obsession: 'Tim, I want to *see* your love for Antony, your huge guilt at his death and your relentless concern with how posterity will view you.'

Here he seems to be pushing his actors towards the excess of which he had spoken. *Antony and Cleopatra* traces the way in which these excesses altered the course of history. The play's epic proportions will only be met if human traits are writ bold – not least so as to make their impact felt in the realms of the Olivier.

Hall also directs attention to those scenes which the run has exposed: some need to be rethought, others have to be reinforced.

At the end of a day's rehearsing, stage management prepares for the first run in the Olivier itself. The great sliding door at the back of Rehearsal Room 1 is opened on to a corridor, and scenery, furniture and props carried through to the lift which transports them up to the stage. Before going on to manage another show that evening, Ernie Hall and his team have still to set things up, and produce the next day's call sheet for distribution to administrative offices and notice boards throughout the building.

WEEK 9 – Run-Through: Part Two

The following morning, the run begins well: the strong martial feel of the opening scene swells with the banner and drum processions. The use of the aisles and balconies extends the space marvellously so that the entire auditorium becomes an arena. Racy, brisk scenes alternate with those that are moody and measured. Hopkins is using his drunkenness selectively – and to greater effect. When he drags in the Schoolmaster with one hand, a wine flagon brandished in the other, we scent the explosion to come.

As Part Two continues, however, the many entrances and exits – taken at a run up and down the aisles, with actors often needing to dash from the back of the auditorium along corridors to the stage – turn into a scramble so that the energy with which the act started, dissipates. Tony Hopkins increasingly needs prompts, sometimes line by line. He and Bryant have four *Lear* performances this week and sound tired. Once more, the 'muscle' of individual scenes has been buried. Can it be redefined?

Afterwards Hall says, 'I wanted to get the physical measure of Act II, the use of the auditorium, of problems like the steps, noisy shoes, talking in the background, the squeaky doors. . . .

'As far as the language is concerned, there are two main areas of concern: every time there's a full stop, there should be a change of tone – we're making it too unvaried, too even. Also, I am now convinced that, on a half-line cue, both the metre and the tone of the previous speaker must be taken over. For example:

> CLEOPATRA .... I little thought
>   You would have followed.
> ANTONY   Egypt, thou knewst too well. . . .

Tony, catch Judi's rhythm and vocal timbre, then work into your own. It focuses the sense.

'It was a muddle today. As you start to act, you lose the form. We'll need to etch the colours of scenes far more deeply. . . . From your point of view, this is a very difficult show technically, so it has to get worse before it gets better. We must make the exits precise. We'll get much sharper cross-cuts if you speak the first line of each scene over the last line of the scene before – and don't worry about starting to talk as you come down the aisles.

'That said . . . if we can keep our nerve and we don't allow this monster to scare us, I know we'll be all right.' His confidence is genuine – and reassuring. This is a general with faith in his army.

WEEK 10 – Monday 16 March

At the start of the tenth week, Peter Hall is delayed back from a weekend in New York.

As scheduled, Judi Dench had finished her West End run that same weekend. Not insignificantly, only now does she succumb to the flu which she had been staving off the week before. She, too is away on the Monday.

In Hall's absence, Alan Cohen takes rehearsals. The BETA/NT stalemate casts a gloomy shadow: the actors are anxious about their own situations: will the production grind to a halt? Will they be made redundant?

Early on Tuesday morning, Hall comes straight to the theatre from the airport. The energy level rises. Dench is also back and, to measure the 'etching' of the interim days, they run Part Two again.

Afterwards, the director is able to say approvingly: 'We got the battle strategy very clearly this time round. Each time sea/land, fighting on ships/on foot is mentioned, hit the antitheses: bring out the contrast of the strange world of the sea (to which the Romans were unused) against the familiarity of the land.

'But,' he says crisply, 'in connection with Rome we still need to think "businesslike", "efficient", "stoic": it is one of the reasons why Antony is drawn to Egypt, where emotion can be revealed, and why it causes comment when Caesar weeps.'

During the run, Tim Pigott-Smith adds an edge of venom to Caesar and when he calls Antony 'the old ruffian', the ruthless inhumanity of the phrase sends a cold shiver through me. Perhaps this is why I still cannot accept the emotion in his eulogy to Antony after the latter's death – it seems too great a leap. Surely his are crocodile tears? Either Shakespeare has provided an insufficient basis for the adulation, or director and actor are going for an impossible interpretation of the lines. . . .

Anthony Hopkins has stopped what he calls his 'roaring' and, taken in a modulated tone, his anger is far more threatening. (It also seems that work on *Antony and Cleopatra* is having a lateral effect: now splendid in *Lear*, according to Basil Henson, 'He has stopped pushing or breaking up the lines and is beginning to lay back on the role and enjoy it!')

Hall, however, feels that Hopkins has lost his 'dark Welsh moments': 'The oscillations between the reined in and the explosive were a little evened out.' This is interesting: where I admire the actor's greater vocal control, from Hall's point of view there has been a dip in dramatic intensity: how to maintain one without losing the other?

In the armour-dressing scene, too, Hall feels that they have lost the undertones beneath the pretence that all is well, as they lost the sense of the miraculous after Antony's unexpected victory (Act IV Scene 8): 'The trouble with these military scenes is that we get a generalized

"Whoopee! Well done, lads!" and we're off: they have to be differentiated.

'Tony, in Act IV Scene 12, you lost some of the pointing in telling Cleopatra exactly what Caesar's triumph in Rome will mean for her:

> Let him take thee
> And hoist thee up to the shouting plebeians;
> (*pronunciation: plee-bians*)
> . . . most monster-like be shown
> For poor'st diminutives, for dolts, and let
> Patient Octavia plough thy visage up
> With her preparéd nails.

'The effect on Antony of the news of Cleopatra's death is almost a relaxation, an acceptance. Once she is dead, he is unmanned and can go to his own death – and when *she* decides to die ("I have nothing/Of woman in me"), she is unwomaned.

'Judi, when Antony is brought to you in the monument, that worked very well. I really believed in her innate instinct for survival: she would not come down to Antony, would watch him die below (were there no pulley to draw him up) rather than give up her stronghold. When he does die, she protests:

> The crown o'th'earth doth melt. My lord!
> O withered is the garland of the war. . . .

Remember, it's not elegaic. And that last speech ("No more but e'en a woman . . .") is fragmented because she's trying to find a way of coming to terms with grief:

> How do you women?
> What, what, good cheer! Why how now, Charmian?
> My noble girls! Ah women, women, look:
> Our lamp is spent, it's out.

'So make her more of the cornered animal. In the scene with Proculeius, I knew her mind was racing to find a way out. Caesar's courtesy to you is such that you can only meet his hypocrisy with yours: respond in kind until Seleucus drops you in it.'

By now Hall must certainly be feeling the effects of jet-lag, but he drives on relentlessly, starting a read-through of Part One of the play in the late afternoon. The next morning he asks for another run, this time from the top of the play, in order to see the fit of the two halves.

There is an audience of interested parties: Alison Chitty, Malcolm Ranson, Steven Wentworth (lighting), Paul Arditti (sound), Dominic Muldowney (music), Nicki Frei (publicist) and even Jan Younghusband (who has managed time away from scheduling the NT's repertoire).

WEEK 10 – Run-Through: Parts One & Two

The actors make an exhilarated start. Anthony Hopkins is experimenting freely. In their opening scene, he and Judi Dench tussle and go down on the floor so that he is lying astride her, for 'here is my space'. It is a new possibility which Hopkins explores to its limits – since he will not let go of Cleopatra, the two of them roll about on the ground until the other actors onstage are laughing, as is Hall. We get the picture. So do the Roman Ambassadors, who are deeply offended.

Michael Bryant is quite wonderful as Enobarbus, completely the down-to-earth soldier, grinning, scratching himself, yet doing total service to the verse. Each time he does the lines about the meeting of Cleopatra and Antony – when she 'pursed up his heart upon the river of Cydnus' – he seems to invent them anew, and one listens anew. Piling image upon glorious image:

> The barge she sat in, like a burnished throne,
> Burned on the water. The poop was beaten gold:
> Purple the sails and so perfumed that
> The winds were lovesick with them . . .

he draws in for the memorable close:

> Age cannot wither her, nor custom stale
> Her infinite variety. Other women cloy
> The appetites they feed but she makes hungry
> Where most she satisfies . . .

The Roman world, by contrast, is cold and puritanical.

Because of a commitment elsewhere, I am unable to watch the second half. The consensus: it was the best run-through yet – and minutes were knocked off the running time (always a good sign). From taciturn Ernie Hall: 'Now we're cooking!'

On the few occasions when circumstances force me to miss part or all of a rehearsal, I am invariably called to task for it by several members of the cast: 'Where were you? You missed something really good yesterday. You'll notice the difference.' Initially somewhat wary they now accept my presence as part of the background to rehearsals and are intrigued to see how I will record the production and, of course, how they, as individuals, will feature in it.

During the run-through, Dench played Act III Scene 3 – in which she questions the Messenger about Octavia – as though still shattered by the news of Antony's marriage. Doubling back over individual scenes, Hall picks up on this. As Cleopatra received the news a full five scenes before (Act III Scene 5), he is sure that by now she would have pulled herself together. The scene is discussed, then played. Hinged on Cleopatra's renewed confidence, it becomes terribly funny, almost Restoration in lightness and wit.

'I have one thing more to ask him yet . . . all may be well enough,' she muses. . . . The scene modulates to introspection, as does the mood in the rehearsal room. Attention turns to detail. The queen's final lines cause a sudden insecurity in her court: why is she planning to write to Antony in his new-married state? 'It's dodgy stuff,' says Hall. 'If he comes back, they know it'll mean war.' There is a sense of getting closest to the truth in the text. Sudden bouts of laughter relieve intensity – and break the late afternoon stillness in the huge work space.

It is exactly a fortnight before the first public preview. On Ernie Hall's table lies a schedule of work in the Olivier Theatre:

	Thurs. 19 March
9.00 a.m.	Strike *Six Characters*
	Lay *Ant. & Cleo.* tracks and fix down
	Build centre truck on tracks
	Sound console work
1.00 p.m.	Lunch Break
2.00	Continue above
	Understudy Rehearsal *Six Chars.*
4.30	Reset and Stage Check
6.00	Supper Break
7.15	Performance *Six Chars.*

	Friday 20 March
9.00 a.m.	Strike *Six Chars.*
	Set *Ant. & Cleo.* infills, ramp and treads
	Rehearse *Ant. & Cleo.*
1.00 p.m.	Lunch Break
2.00	Continue above
4.30	Strike *Ant. & Cleo.*
	Set *Six Chars.*
6.00	Supper Break
7.15	Performance *Six Chars.*

Once again, screens, doors and props are moved up to the Olivier for Friday's rehearsal. The infills round off the front of the stage, making of it a complete circle and providing the actors with more breadth in which to work.

They work through the play scene by scene. After each, Hall gives notes, the scene's overlap with the next is fine-tuned and then it is re-run. Such is their professionalism, both stage management and actors need only one opportunity to work out these sometimes complex cross-overs: by the re-run, all is efficient execution. Some of the permanent stage crew of the Olivier sit out front in the stalls, observing scenic changes which they take over in the Technical week. Amongst the logistical difficulties in this vast arena (when action on the stage could be inaudible or 'masked' by the mobile sections of the set), is that of timing an entrance: for almost every entrance – be it from 'the wings', from behind the doors onstage, or from the doors at the top of the aisles – Angela Bissett will flash a 'cue light' from her control box at the back of the stalls. (From there, she will also cue the movement of the doors and walls of the set, the carrying on and 'striking' of furniture and props, sound effects, smoke effects and lighting changes.) As they occur in rehearsing, she marks up all these cues.

On the stage itself, Hall is encouraging clearer moves and gestures, a more emphatic planting of information and taking of pauses. He directs Mike Hayward in his opening speech to 'Take in the whole audience, with Brian (Spink's) eye as your reference'. In the scene between Caesar and Lepidus, he now has the Messengers come in through the auditorium, seeming to bombard them with information. When Antony first meets Caesar, he tells Hopkins to posture more. ('You're the charmer, the man of honour, the good husband – a richer colouring will contrast with Tim's introversion.') To Pigott-Smith himself he gives an overt action for 'You have broken/The article of your oath . . .': he is to stand up, then subside back into his seat. The actor is several times advised: 'This stage pulls you forward. Don't be tempted.' (The focal point of the Olivier stage, the area from which to dominate it, is in fact centred about a third of the distance from the front. When an actor comes right downstage – as does Hopkins after his humiliating flight from Actium, and Bryant for Enobarbus' death scene – he becomes very exposed and vulnerable; it is also a position from which to establish intimacy with the audience.)

Hall and Alan Cohen constantly check 'sightlines', the audience view of the action, from all over the fan-shaped auditorium, repositioning screens and actors so that no one will be masked.

Certain scenes are restaged in these final weeks. Sometimes this is because the transfer from rehearsal room to theatre has highlighted problems – of masking or sheer territory to be covered. More often, though, it is to take advantage of the opportunities offered by the space – its generous width and depth, its aisles and balconies – the more amply to communicate Shakespeare's 'most spacious of plays'.

Hall has been concerned about two scenes in particular: the meeting between the Triumvirate and Pompey, and that on Pompey's galley: today he radically alters both.

First, the screens are completely retracted, so that the whole expanse of the stage is bared. Then the full length of the Olivier, stage and auditorium, is exploited: Pompey and his men come down the centre aisle and up on to the stage, to meet face on with Caesar, Lepidus and Antony, who have themselves advanced down the centre of the stage, followed by Agrippa, Maecenas, a standard bearer and three drummers. This invasion of territory from points furthest apart is full of power. The clash of war seems imminent. The tension holds – and then is defused: at precisely the same moment the opposing leaders exchange deep Renaissance bows. The two groups wheel to either side of the stage and prepare to negotiate.

After a reconciliation has been effected, an en masse exit is made up the centre aisle, supposedly towards Pompey's galley. For the next scene, they come back down this aisle to mount the stage – which is now the galley.

Whilst Caesar, Agrippa and Maecenas weave their way round the tables to their seats, Antony and Lepidus are isolated downstage for all the initial business about the 'flow o'th' Nile', crocodiles and 'pyramises': Lepidus doggedly pursues the subject, circling in on Antony to clutch at him with each slurred query. Enobarbus hovers irritably, ever protective of his master, whilst Pompey, propped against the opposite corner of the table, watches malevolently, urging his servants to refill Lepidus' glass. It is from here that Menas draws Pompey downstage to suggest cutting his opponents' throats. Then Lepidus is carried off drunk, up the aisle. By bringing the action closer to the audience and physically delineating the separate strands of the scene, its menacing sub-text has surfaced.

The director is somewhat in the position of the writer whose characters take over, revealing possibilities of which he had not conceived. By freely restaging, Hall triggers a new spurt of inventiveness from his actors: Hopkins, who has been worried that this scene was flaccid, now becomes the life and soul of the party, going for an explicit display of debauchery. After they have danced 'the Egyptian bacchanals' he falls to the ground, pulling down Tim Pigott-Smith and, satyr-like, entangling limbs with him. (This gives Caesar ample cause for 'Good brother, Let me request you off'.) Next he lurches round the table after Caesar who grabs a stool in fury, to fend him off. Finally, with 'Give's your hand', he challenges Pompey and yanks him over the table, to end with his foot on the fallen man's chest.

Once again, the actor has captured Antony's abandoned recklessness. Prepared to go further than anyone in experimental playfulness, he is carrying the risks for them all – and forcing the scene towards an unpredictable edge. (He has always been somewhat nervous about displaying sexuality on stage; by releasing him to explore extremes – the licence and indiscriminate bisexuality of early Rome – he says that *Antony and Cleopatra* has helped him to break through that boundary.)

To make up for the Monday when Hall was away, the company is called in on Saturday – and again do a run of the play.

One can feel the electricity, the powerful attraction between Antony and Cleopatra. Dench has become increasingly sensuous, coiling herself round Antony, clinging to him, very aware of his physical presence (and hungry for it in his absence).

At the news of Antony's marriage, she howls with primary pain. That, each time the scene is run, she is able to release it so fully and with such dramatic exactness, is not something tumbled to by chance; a whole career in the theatre has built towards it (and film and television work, which came later, would not have equipped her equally). 'Quantity is the practice that makes quality perfect', wrote Kenneth Tynan of Olivier's prolific output on stage. Depth of experience and mastery of technique combine with Dench's unique inborn qualities to serve a startling communication of feelings.

Interestingly, now that the scene on Pompey's galley has been restaged, each of the actors finally locks into his own particular form of drunkenness: John Bluthal sways on his feet, has trouble enunciating, Basil Henson and Graham Sinclair chortle together, one whoozy, the other hiccuping mildly, Michael Bryant's Enobarbus is amiable – and falling over. Pigott-Smith's Caesar is peevish and unhappy; he has to be persuaded to indulge and struggles to maintain his dignity. David Schofield becomes the malicious, spiteful drinker. The hardheaded clarity of Michael Carter's Menas, who alone has abstained, stands out.

In this man's world, where the weak are carelessly disposed of, Octavia's vulnerability is thrown into sharp relief. Her return to her brother ends with Sally Dexter and Tim Pigott-Smith centre stage, clasped in one another's arms; in the break before they continue with Part Two, Hall tells them: 'You've now truly justified the placing of the interval.'

This second half goes at a rattling pace: the groups of soldiers, marching and in ceremonial attendance, provide a vivid sense of the machinery of war.

As Antony declines, Cleopatra's continuing staunchness seems remarkable: this is clearly a harsh, opportunistic world where it is romantic folly to remain loyal if it is not in your interests – Enobarbus' dilemma.

One truly feels for Antony at Enobarbus' desertion – and for his generosity of spirit: 'My fortunes have corrupted honest men. . . .' There is great warmth and fellowship, too, for Eros in their final scene together.

Dench is fully in command of Act V: steadfast, pitiable, ultimately ennobled – and touching in the scene with the Clown (whom John Bluthal renders human and earthy).

I feel that, were the company to go no further, they have made an 'arrival' – the play is deeply satisfying.

Giving notes, Hall is sympathetic: 'It's like taking on two plays – Part One and Part Two – the size is awesome.'

He gives detailed line readings, planting key words: to Mike Bottle, bringing news of Menas and Menecrates: '"*Pirates*" – give them their billing!'; to Hopkins: '"I am not married, Caesar" is almost the most awful of Antony's lines. Let plenty of air in around it'; and to Jerry Flynn: '"Free madam! . . . He's bound unto Octavia". Connect that "free" and "bound".') On the other hand: 'This doesn't apply to you, Judi, Tony, Michael, but everyone else can now relax deliberately on the text. It's still slightly dutiful. . . . Can it be fleeter, lighter, wittier? We don't want the audience to feel they're being lectured to. . . .'

Once more, he stresses the super-courtesy of the Triumvirate towards Pompey: 'Having emerged from the Wars of the Roses, Shakespeare and the Elizabethans feared civil war above all things,' and warns against 'the generalized military brisk' of 'Shakespearean war acting'.

For Michael Bryant, some fresh perceptions: 'I think your growing determination to leave Antony should be less reflective, more impatient and angry. Antony is becoming paranoid and absurd, Cleopatra is apparently flirting her way into a peace with Caesar. . . .' ('No wonder I leave,' growls Bryant. 'I'm with a bunch of loonies, traitors, weirdos, pinkos, commies. . . .')

'Tony and Tim,' continues Hall. 'Be more specifically right-wing, dislike change and the populace. We have an inbuilt belief in the common man. Those people didn't. They were ruthless in their exploitation and self-aggrandisement: it's a world of "survival of the fittest".

'The play is becoming shocking, which I find exciting. It's about two people who, despite the romantic mythology, were totally self-indulgent and egocentric, and Caesar, a monstrous opportunist who disgracefully used the precepts of ancient Rome for his own ends. You must race ahead of the audience, shock them into thinking about the realities of power, confuse them by exposing the two sides of Antony and Cleopatra, the repellent as well as the attractive and endearing.' (This anarchic romanticism has many modern parallels: it was no coincidence that, as I watched the central duo in Shakespeare's play during this run, I kept thinking of George and Martha in *Who's afraid of Virginia Woolf?*')

The play is moving towards another revelation which pleases Hall. It relates to the survival versus suicide paradox he discussed with Dench – and which the writing sets up: 'After the death of Antony, the audience should fear that Cleopatra might be corrupt and live, because they are actually waiting for her to die – and honourably.'

WEEK 11 – Monday 23 March

At the start of the eleventh week, the pace is still calm and steady. From now on, the actors become increasingly reliant on the director's judgement: they are solidly grounded in their characters, but he is the one 'out there' and in a position to orchestrate the interplay between them. By this stage Hall is expressing crystallized views on the play's many themes, and the statement being made in each scene. Nevertheless, his method of direction continues to be one of suggestion and quiet persistence.

There is lengthy discussion about Act IV Scene 2, for example, the scene with the servants. Hopkins feels that he can only convey Antony's acute self-pity if it arises out of a far-gone inebriation. Although Hall has by this time realized that the scene works best, dramatically, if Antony is sober and tragically self-aware, at no point does he impose his view – he waits for the actor to arrive at the conclusion himself.

Beneath the calm, tension and excitement are rising: this is the final week of pure rehearsal before technical aspects of the show are introduced. Sitting in the canteen with the entire cast filling one of the long tables, Peter Hall reminisces about working through the night on technical rehearsals when he was at the RSC. Judi Dench, too, remembers emerging from them at dawn. Anna Massey and other colleagues stop at the table to congratulate her for receiving the British Film and Television Academy award for Best Supporting Actress in *A Room With a View*. She still has not seen it, as neither she nor Antony Hopkins have yet seen *84 Charing Cross Road*, in which they play husband and wife, and which has a Royal Command Performance that night.

Technical elements begin to make themselves felt: in the Olivier,

Stephen Wentworth is trying out lighting for the battle of Actium. Canidius (Dan Thorndike) and several soldiers are deployed on the balcony to the right of the stalls. A 'follow spot' will isolate Enobarbus onstage, as he looks out into the auditorium, following the battle's progress. Then the lights will come up on the men in the balcony.

Hopkins' armour is available for him to work in: a Roman tunic with epaulettes and skirt panels, made of calfskin. The tunic has yet to be dyed and ornamented with bronze and leather but when the actor reclines, testing for flexibility, he does indeed look like a figure from a Titian painting. The armour-dressing scene can now be dealt with practically. Dench and Jerry Flynn work out the timing and complexities of buckling on the tunic, attaching arm and leg greaves.

For the opening of the play, Frances Quinn and Peter Gordon – as attendants – now have large palm fronds to wave. Also ready for use in the rehearsal room are tall standards, made up of wreaths attached to cross-pieces.

Malcolm Ranson choreographs Cleopatra's attempt to stab herself, which Proculeius blocks: as ever, he removes the mystique, breaking the moves down into several stages, his first concern being the safety of the actors. (Worried about Dench's intended jump from the monument, he has suggested a net covered by a carpet, into which she can fall.)

Meanwhile, there is something of a crisis with the central door-cum-monument structure: the machinery to telescope one out of the other is not fitting into the doorframe . . . which must now be reassembled.

The National has the most up-to-date sound equipment, tailored to its needs. The console, or control desk, at the back of the Olivier stalls, for instance, was built to specifications. Seated at it, Paul Arditti talks about the sound requirements of the play, especially those for the sea battles: 'There is library material of wind, crashing waves, battle cries and explosions, from the theatre's tape archive – but it can sound artificial. We are going for something between the literal and the extraordinary. The battles at sea should assault the audience with cataclysmic noise.' He is working closely with Dominic Muldowney on a mixture of digital sounds and they have been experimenting with a synthesizer. Arditti speaks with fervour about the importance of sound 'design', of marrying it to the overall concept of a production, as is the design of the set or lighting.

Muldowney himself joined the National in 1976 (for Peter Hall's production of *Tamburlaine the Great*), replacing Harrison Birtwhistle as Director of Music in 1981. Besides writing the music for innumerable NT productions, he has composed for ballet and television, and for films such as *Betrayal*, *The Ploughman's Lunch* and *1984*. His concert works are featured at the Festival Hall and the Proms, and he has a growing interest in music-theatre.

As early as the third week of rehearsal, Peter Hall compiled a brief of the music he wanted for *Antony and Cleopatra*. The memo Muldowney received detailed every music cue – something he had never had before – and has led to the instrumentation as it is. 'Hall understands music,' says the composer. 'He not only puts a lot of faith in it, for his productions, but he's able to be specific about changes.'

The director had included a request for 'a sound to silence the audience at the beginning of the play': Muldowney thought of 'grains of sand in the North African desert'. He and Arditti have produced what the latter calls a 'cosmic drone' from part of a note played on an oboe: dropped in pitch, it is then multiplied electronically and endlessly extended (or 'looped').

Knowing that this was the classical world seen through Renaissance eyes, Muldowney kept in mind what someone in 1607 would do if they were writing music for the play. Accordingly, there are no instruments used, from Europe or the Arabic/North African world, that are not of that period, and he and the National's Music Manager, Kevin Leeman, have had to find musicians able to play such instruments.

For the first time, these musicians are on hand to rehearse with the actors. Heralding the banquet scene on Pompey's galley, the two trumpeters produce a splendid sound which echoes round the Olivier: the radio mikes they carry feed their notes back to the sound console at the rear of the stalls, where Arditti amplifies the music and adds reverberation. Similarly, the music made onstage by the fiddle, crumhorn, tambourine and zitar (a French medieval stringed instrument with a long fret) can be mixed, brought up or taken down at the console. It is an evocative combination which accompanies the men's dance and then the song. The haunting melody for 'Cup us till the world go round' is carried, in pure, high voices, by two young schoolboys, Peter Corey and Paul Vinhas, who will do alternate performances. Standing on the tables, amidst actors and musicians, they sing with complete professional composure.

'*Antony and Cleopatra* is not difficult to write music for,' contends Muldowney. 'But those fanfares have been done to death. By using "reverb", you get something new which serves several purposes: it gives you a sense of the vast world of Shakespeare's imagining, it gives a modern feel to those authentic notes and rhythms – and it fills the Olivier space.'

Two days later, the same musicians are at rehearsals with instruments for the Egyptian court: hand-drums, two Egyptian trumpets, a bombard (with its bagpipe sound), an oud (an Arabic lute) and a narrow fiddle, the rebec, of medieval English origin. Now the music has a distinctly Middle Eastern sinuousness, with a strong rhythmic base. Before the opening sequence of the play is rehearsed, Hall talks to the musicians about the looser ambiance of the Egyptian scenes.

Music cues throughout the play are gone through, and decisions made about where the musicians are to be placed: Pompey will be heralded by trumpets and triple drums from the ramps connecting side aisles and stage. The two lone notes of Renaissance trumpets will be sounded onstage for the Triumviral meetings. At other times, trumpets will call from the back of the auditorium, or the balconies.

'This is a lean production,' says the composer. 'I've tried to exclude everything which intrudes on the narrative.' For him, as for designers Alison Chitty and Stephen Wentworth, watching rehearsals is a constant guideline and stimulus.

WEEK 11 – Run-Through: Complete Play

The Olivier is teeming with actors, musicians, the boy-singers and their headmaster/chaperon, sound and lighting technicians, stage staff and Cynthia Goodall from Wardrobe with a pile of boots for the men. ASM Paul Greaves has his prompt script set up on a lectern in the front row of the stalls.

Hall prepares the company for the first complete run-through in the theatre – and the last opportunity to concentrate on performance unencumbered by technical complexities: 'Go out and bite it. Splash about in the Olivier. . . .'

It has been a week with an unspoken sense of the structure of the play locking into place. The mood is one of energy and optimism. At 10.45 a.m. the run-through begins. Dench, with a dagger on her hip, has the feline swagger of a manipulative and seductive woman. She has opened up her movements to take in the breadth of the stage. Antony has constantly to curb her: as had been proposed at the start of rehearsals, 'she runs circles round him and he loves it'.

The actors playing smaller parts all deliver forcibly. Iain Ormsby-Knox has defined Mardian: underpinning the dignity, his hand movements and voice express innuendo and wit. Miranda Foster radiates vitality (confidence vastly increased by David Hare's praise of her Cordelia, after he returned from a five-month absence in New York). And it is as if Jerry Flynn has whipped the covers off his careful construction of Eros: suddenly, a whole personality is convincingly there – boyish, earnest, loyal, charming.

After the grotesque bacchanalia on Pompey's galley, the stage is wiped with sombre grandeur for the aftermath of battle in Parthia: Muldowney's echoing funeral march as the body of Pacorus is borne in, Brian Spink's measured tones, the military ranks standing to attention and – a recent addition to the scene – the still presence of Daniel Thorndike in the background, as a priest presiding over a sacrificial pyre, all have an awesome theatrical power. The victory over the Parthians has been made duly momentous, and acid comparison drawn between the leaders of the Empire and their generals. Strange to think that, in productions of the play, this scene is often omitted.

In the second half of the play, Hopkins' Antony comes across as a fallen colossus, a figure of tragedy. As his curve of power plummets, that of Octavius Caesar builds relentlessly. Pigott-Smith develops from wavering pupil to ruthless politician. The cross-over is dramatic.

In a newly-invented moment at the end, Dench shows both Cleopatra's instinct for survival and her vulnerability: she actually clasps Caesar's hand while kneeling before him, and we wonder whether she is wavering, whether she *is* resolved to die. . . .

The death scene, when it comes (and the garter snake is used – and behaves), has everyone in the auditorium watching in suspense.

As to whether the throne, with Cleopatra dead upon it, will be processed up the centre aisle or carried back through the monument, Hall is still unsure. He sits on the edge of the stage to give his notes, the actors in the stalls before him.

'There's one thing I'll try to say about the next jump the play must take, but it's hard. It is about the sensual nature of language. . . . For me, when Shakespeare works, it's when you feel he's inventing these extraordinary metaphors and images out of deep emotion, physicalized in words, words which you can taste, smell, touch. . . . I don't know if it happens intellectually or emotionally.

'Sometimes in your performance the language goes like electricity; at other times it's a bit dry – you have to make the text more new-minted, more necessary, more conjured up.

'At the moment, we have a freely-staged play which grew out of feeling. Now we'll be adding costumes and set which have a pictorial eloquence. Pragmatic work will be needed, once I see you out there, under the lights. Although your costumes will make you feel good, you'll need to make an adjustment: Renaissance dress is all about "making a show". With figures in costume against a one-toned set, we will need to think consciously about the images. Try to define the picture you're making. In relation to one another, wherever Cleopatra moves, the court moves with her. The Romans stand their ground.'

The Technical is called for the following Tuesday. (The first public preview will be four days later.) Hall's final words before the weekend break are cautionary: 'Do take care of yourselves on every level. I don't want to flog you all next week so that you're on your knees by Friday's Preview. . . .' He had described Technicals as 'a test of endurance, patience and tenacity'; I wait to discover how exhausting a week it will be. . . .

CHAPTER 10

The Technical – 'a Test of Endurance, Patience and Tenacity'

WEEK 12 – Monday 30 March

For the final production week of *Antony and Cleopatra*, the Olivier Theatre is closed to the public. The set of *Six Characters in Search of an Author* is moved into a scene dock, behind metal shutters at the back of the Olivier stage, to clear the stage for the incoming play.

With Production Manager Michael Cass Jones and his assistant George Ellerington in overall charge, the team of fifteen stage technicians, led by Dennis Nolan, two power-flying operators (who control the stage revolve and raise and lower pulleys and lighting 'cradles' or 'ladders' from high above the stage) and the Head of Lighting Peter Radmore and his electricians, work through Monday 30 March on the fit-up. The props team, under John Pursey, carry the props onstage from either rehearsal room or workshop and set them up, supervised by Emma Lloyd, using the setting lists she has prepared. Ernie Hall and his stage managers will hand over the shifting of set, furniture and props to the Olivier's permanent stage staff during the technical run.

By Tuesday morning (with infills in place to round off the stage and ramps providing access from stage to aisles), the massive circular floor is down, its closely-fitting panels laid according to a numbered floor plan. Also firmly secured are the tracks along which the set will move forward and back, by means of steel cables connected to winching mechanisms. The thirty-metre expanse of cyclorama – hundreds of sturdy ties attaching it to a support rail – has been hoisted up on pulleys dropped from the flies. Floor and backcloth provide a great swathe of glowing colour; the effect is of ox-blood stucco. Walls and door section are in place, mounted on wheeled trucks. Immensely tall and slightly concave, each wall has been constructed in two sections, a pedimented top projecting beyond a base supporting slab onto which it has been lowered. The join between the two halves on each wall has yet to be concealed and the crumbling stonework surrounding the huge central doors is still in the process of being painted: but here, in all but final detail, is the ruined Renaissance edifice of Alison Chitty's conceiving.

With over 450 lamps rigged for use in the Olivier, as far as possible Stephen Wentworth has avoided changing the position of those already being used for productions with which *Antony and Cleopatra* will alternate on the same stage. Additional lights, specific to this production, can be rigged or re-focused with relative speed, since, in 1986, a three-dimensional 'bridge' was installed high up in the flies above the stage. Wentworth and Chitty have communicated constantly whilst she designed the set. During run-throughs, he has made notes and diagrams of where actors were standing, the possible lighting effect to aim for during a scene, and the point at which it would change to a different effect. More recently, Hall has talked to him about the Renaissance quality of the production, the warmth of lighting needed for the scenes in Egypt, and the cool colours and sharp definition needed for Rome. The lamps being used have been fitted with gelatine squares (gels) to produce the appropriate contrasts of colour.

Although eventually the lighting of the show will be run from the control box at the back of the stalls, for the week of technical rehearsals Wentworth works from a console set up in the auditorium. He is now ready to build up a lighting 'state' for each section of the play, detail each 'cue' (change of lighting), and feed them into the computer beside him. He can vary the pace, so as to go from one state to another in three seconds, or four, or six. With great freedom to be inventive, he will try to capture emotion and mood rather than an effect which is literal.

By 2.00 p.m. on Tuesday, Hall is able to tell the cast assembled in the Olivier auditorium that 'the stage is ahead of itself. Let's get on with the technical. You've an hour to get ready. . . .' He also says something he will repeat during the week: 'This is the first time in my life I've had enough time on a play and I'm not going to throw it away now. Let's see how we go. If we're not ready by Friday, we'll postpone the first Previews.' It may relieve the pressure on cast and crew, but the administrative implications torment Nicki Frei. There are some questions about make-up for those in Egypt. How dark should it be? Chitty has left sticks of burnished colour in the dressing-rooms. As they walk round the stage before going to get dressed, Hall comments: 'The Olivier hates noise.' Hopkins assesses his surroundings: 'I won't be able to throw *this* set around. . . .'

By 3.00 the actors start to trickle back, to present themselves to director and designer. The costumes are breathtaking: the actors are delighted and swirl about, getting the feel of them on the stage. John Bluthal is resplendent in grey shot-silk breeches and quilted, broad-shouldered doublet. A pale grey and gold cloak, fixed across his chest, falls to the floor in formal folds. With his grey hair powdered and brushed forward in a Roman curled fringe, he embodies Trium-viral pomp and dignity. Anthony Hopkins and Judi Dench wear open caftans, with pointed and tasselled sleeves. Richly brocaded, his is worn over a soft, full shirt, tucked into his breeches, hers over an ivory-coloured dress, waisted and low-necked, its bodice embroi-dered and beaded. She is utterly transformed by a mane of long auburn curls, which leaves her forehead clear. Her attendant women, too, are in wigs of tawny ringlets. Their dresses, in pinky-beige, grey and pale coffee shades, have panelled skirts, through which show soft underdresses in darker tones, giving a pantaloon effect when they sit. On their feet are pointed velvet slippers. Alexas (Bob Arnold) is in caftan and turban. The eunuchs (Ormsby-Knox and Peter Gordon) wear head-hugging gold helmets; full-length coats reveal bare chests, wide cummerbunds and brilliant blue trousers gathered at the ankle. The wardrobe staff are on hand to pin, adjust the hang of cloaks, note alterations. Seeing the figures against the monumental set for the first time, the proportions are marvellously 'epic'.

Angie Bissett, in headphones up in her control box, communicates with Ernie Hall and Emma Lloyd, in similar headphones, down on the stage. On her three-ring intercom system, she is also in touch with the men winching the walls and doors, with the two lighting operators in the box near hers, those on the follow-spots and those pumping smoke on to the stage from the 'vomitories' beneath the front of the stage on either side, and with Paul Arditti at his sound console. Ernie Hall will give actors their calls from his tannoying point stage left. When a scene change is due, Bissett will give a standby call to everyone concerned, including actors making an entrance, and then a light for the cue itself. Once the play opens, she will also give the front-of-house calls summoning the audience to their seats.

A decision must be made about the opening configuration of doors and walls, the 'pre-set' which will greet this incoming audience. Hall at first orchestrates a build-up; houselights go down, the set moves forward, the 'cosmic drone' is heard and then the actors enter. Later, he is to decide that this is too 'busy'. Doors and walls are pre-set downstage in an interlocked semi-circle, creating substance and stillness, which the drone reinforces.

Once they start to work through the play, the actors show an obvious response to being in costume. Tony Hopkins swaggers about in his full-length robe, flaunting the soft eastern garment before the Romans in their sombre ambassadorial splendour. Tim Pigott-Smith, wearing a midnight blue, gold-bordered cloak over silver and blue striped doublet and breeches, makes an arresting first entrance. A fringed hairpiece, blending with the reddish tone of his own hair, makes him look ten years younger, arrogant and tight-braced. David Schofield strides gleefully through the auditorium, a high-voltage figure in black leather, gauntleted hands held high, an emerald cloak billowing behind him. Sally Dexter sails across the stage, skirt full-gathered at the back, an elaborately coiled wig adding to her stateliness. Jerry Flynn is immediately at home in suede boots, wide velvet breeches and doublet. Beneath his dark curly hair, a gold ring gleams from one ear: he typifies youthful Renaissance energy.

In designing the costumes, Alison Chitty has extended the personality of each actor to mesh with the character they play: Bryant/ Enobarbus is unembellished, in workmanlike brown leather doublet and dark breeches. Bearded for Ventidius, Brian Spink is a figure of imposing dignity in maroon and black. Basil Henson's own taut presence is drawn on for Caesar's general – white hair combed forward to accentuate a naturally stern profile, he is in dark green, bands of gold braid cutting across his doublet – and later, when Andrew Wadsworth appears as the courtier Dolabella, his leonine blondness is enhanced by an extravagant sky-blue cloak over a beribboned costume of the same colour.

Occasionally, as they go from scene to scene, a wall section is winched in too quickly and collides with the advancing doors. Since each piece advances to a given number, and can move at one of three speeds – fast, medium or slow – adjustments can be made so that the action is controlled. Each time the sections jam, Ernie Hall and Cass-Jones move in to assess damage, and the changeover between scenes is re-run, several times if necessary.

Co-ordination of all the effects requires remarkable precision and sensitivity. There is a clear division of responsibility: leaving the relevant staff to sort out the technical hitches, Peter Hall conserves his energies to concentrate on the creative assembly of effects. It is obvious, in this final week, that he has a very specific idea of what he wants to achieve, and is quietly relentless about getting there: in the process of integrating the physical aspects of the production, he is harnessing them to the clarity of the story, the tension and excite-ment of its onward flow.

Sometimes seated at a desk half-way back in the stalls with Alan Cohen, more often standing in the centre aisle, he constantly urges Angie Bissett to 'cue quicker'. As the last line of a scene is delivered, the doors should already be moving forward, with the actors coming through them or charging down the aisles, heralded by trumpet calls or sound effects, for the next scene.

In time with this, the lighting will move from one state to another: Wentworth experiments, adding or subtracting colour and intensity, according to suggestions made by Hall: 'Can we spotlight the Messenger on that ramp? Give us a cooler spread of colour in this scene.'

There is a problem with the audience sightlines on the three chairs in the Triumviral conferences. Hall and Cohen go up on to the stage to try different placings – further downstage? In a straight line? (In this production, all the furniture is in fact brought onstage by actors playing soldiers or servants in the scene concerned: they receive a nominal fee – a 'Pickfords' – for the task.) At Pompey's first entrance, there is a combination of taped and live drum-rolls: the sounds are not distant enough, feels Hall, and Paul Arditti and Muldowney work together on getting the desired effect. Also dissat-isfied with the use being made of the weapon rack upstage – 'That grouping is horrible!' – the director moves in to rearrange it.

The actors, when not in a scene, sit about in the auditorium gloriously garbed. Onstage, Judi Dench's inventiveness continues: in the 'Give me some music' scene, as the musicians strike up and Mardian starts to sing, she begins a sinuous dance. There are wholly new inflections, new thinking, behind some of her lines: this is the first time, for instance, that she chokes on saying 'Octavia', a reaction which comes from the gut.

The confrontation between the Triumvirate and Pompey, recently restaged, is now superbly theatrical. The changeover into this scene, with its complex cueing of set movement, sound, lighting and actors' entrances, is re-run five times before the director is completely satisfied. Organizing most of the grouping of the soldiers, Alan Cohen seems to know Hall's requirements intuitively. Highly confident about using the Olivier stage (for which he directed *The Pied Piper*), he is invaluable when it comes to resolving its logistical problems.

In the late afternoon David Aukin, Executive Director of the NT, drops in. In the upper level of the stalls, there is a growing crowd of onlookers, some office staff, various members of the costume department and a group of dressers. (The leading actors have their own dressers, whilst for the smaller roles, a single dresser is shared amongst four or five actors each of whom might in fact have several rapid changes.) When, at one point, a buzz of conversation and laughter rises from this area, Hall raises his voice: 'Quiet up there. We *are* trying to work.' In eleven and a half weeks this is the first instance of impatience that I have seen. Silence falls.

For Pompey's galley a heavy pulley is dropped from the flies carrying two sets of rope rigging, each weighted by a wooden beam. Actors have carried in the pine tables, loaded with stools, ornamental stands of fruit and lanterns, from either side of the stage. On their way out, they pull a set of ropes taut to left and right of the stage, hooking the beams to the floor itself so as to frame the tables with a 'tent' of rigging. Rapidly conferring with Alison Chitty, Hall decides that the walls are no longer needed to enclose this scene. The musicians are grouped in the shadows upstage. At the moment when most of the revellers are seated and platters of risotto are carried in, I experience a complete 'sense of place': the encircling darkness of night, faces illuminated by lanterns, an undertone of talk and laughter breaking through the stillness that one gets near water . . . one almost expects to hear the lapping of waves! It has the quality of a Caravaggio painting.

From where I sit there is a distinct smell of freshly-worked leather as a group of soldiers wait to march down the centre aisle. They wear grey-dyed leather tunics buckled over ochre-coloured breeches and doublets, helmets of calfskin over fibreglass.

Tim Pigott-Smith comes onstage in gold gloves. Alison Chitty, in amazement: 'Who gave you those?' The actor (as if it's contagious): 'Agrippa's got them, too. Want to see my helmet?' As he puts it on, it sinks halfway down his nose – 'He ruled the known world, would you believe!' He is in ebullient good humour: later, when a Messenger's entrance is delayed in the middle of a scene, he starts to improvise:

> I'd as lief have a throsset in a bumble bush
> As a bent reed splashing about in the thickets.
> Oh fortune doth begin to muck about with me,
> Where *is* he?

There is a problem when he has to climb the metal ladder to the balcony in his leather battledress. Should he put it on in the quick-change room up in the balcony? Can Graham Sinclair (Taurus) catch the scroll which Pigott-Smith throws down, against the light and whilst looking through the leather straps of his visor? Ernie Hall: 'Stephen, can we have a light in the stage right corner? There's a congestion problem: those soldiers exiting with banners can't see where they're going. . . .'

Wednesday, 1 April. The Tech. continues. It gives a vivid view of the complexity and scale of a 'national' production: there are so many forces converging on the Olivier, so many people contributing their skills. Weeks of industry in the rehearsal room have produced an illumination of the text and performances of a stature quite equal to the majesty of the set, the rich costuming and emotive music. To hand are the most sophisticated staging facilities of subsidized British theatre; this is the crucial process of integrating art and technology.

The noise of the battle of Actium echoes round the auditorium, heard by most of us for the first time. One is caught up in a maelstrom of crashing waves, the boom of explosions and chilling cries. Lighting plays across the cyclorama with the effect of leaping red flames, as if reflected from the sea, and smoke pours from the 'vomitories' on either side of the stage (extruded from smoke guns in which compressed oil is passed over a heated element).

For the next scene, Dench is in a heavy, gold-embossed war robe, her women wear 'martial' shawls, draped, Amazon-like, across one shoulder. Moving forward, they make a sorrowful swish.

The doors advance for the nightwatch scene. Soldiers wrapped in cloaks, carrying halberds and, in some cases, lanterns, spread out across the stage and into the aisles. They stand, etched against the backdrop, halberds extended. Hall: 'Stephen, touch them in with light. Make it stronger on the one who is speaking.' For the 'music i'th'air', the haunting sound of the cor anglais replicates the 'hautboys' of the script: of necessity pre-recorded, each phrase comes from a different source, using the loudspeakers placed all over the theatre, and starting under the stage itself. The soldiers switch direction to follow its course. Arditti and Muldowney experiment with different sound levels until the effect is remote and mystical.

So-called 'quick changes' cause almost inevitable hold-ups. Dressers and actors are having to adjust to unfamiliar costumes: repetition will speed things up. There is a break when the door and wall sections jam again. Judi Dench, looking thoughtful and a bit sad, reclines on the stage. Near her, gesturing sharply, her face animated, Miranda Foster talks intensely to Iain Ormsby-Knox. He listens in silence, nods in sympathy.

Hall and Hopkins are sitting one behind the other in the front rows of the stalls. Killing time, Hopkins to Hall: 'They like all that, the audience? Us running through the auditorium?' The director: 'Some do. Others find it a bit intimidating, it makes them feel smaller. . . .'

At 5.00, Enobarbus' death scene having been done, Ernie Hall gives the actor an official release: 'Thank you very much, Michael.' He gets an envious farewell from those left behind.

The central structure is opened up to form the monument. At 6.00, Cass-Jones and several technicians make use of the supper break to test the movement of the pulley projecting from the top of it.

At 7.00, those involved start work on Antony's final scene. Judi Dench, Foster, Fitzgerald and Ormsby-Knox negotiate their way up the metal ladder, and through a trapdoor to the balcony of the monument.

Malcolm Ranson is onstage. Tony Hopkins, with a halter round his waist, hangs on to the rope suspended from the pulley and is drawn up by those on the balcony. Helped by Dench, he uses his legs to clamber over the balustrade: the effect is not entirely satisfactory. After several trial ascents, he too is free to go home.

Ranson has brought in Tim Condren, a stuntman who normally works on films, to work out Cleopatra's descent from the monument. He takes things slowly and with extreme caution. A pile of mattresses are placed where Dench will land; two soldiers will lower her from the balcony, two below will catch hold of her feet, she will fall forward into the arms of four more. Everything stops whilst Cass-Jones climbs up to the balcony to saw off an entire section of balustrade so that she can sit on the edge of it, and while he attaches handholds to the back wall.

Sally Dexter, watching from the auditorium, suddenly rushes forward and flings herself on to the mattresses, bouncing up and down. All the surrounding soldiers tumble inwards like ninepins. Laughter relieves the tension – and the tedium.

Condren makes the first descent himself. Then Judi Dench, who has changed into a tracksuit, tries it. There are several seconds when she is breathlessly suspended by the arms, her feet barely reaching the waiting hands below – then she drops into the midst of the support group and comes up beaming, to a round of applause. She repeats the fall with growing confidence, until it is safe for the mattresses to be removed. At 10.45 p.m., Ernie Hall calls an end to a long day.

By 11.00 the next morning, they are back to continue. John Bluthal, in rough-textured robes and sandals, a dark beard framing his jaw, could be a figure out of a nineteenth-century painting of the Holy Land.

Cleopatra's death scene is a series of logistical obstacles. The throne is carried to the front of the monument. Helen Fitzgerald collects the voluminous gold robe. Chitty shows her how to prepare it so as to slip it over Dench's outstretched arms with minimal delay. Miranda Foster finds it difficult to place the elaborate gold crown on Dench's head whilst standing behind her. Then the garter snake proves over-active and Cleopatra (supposedly dead) giggles helplessly as it slithers down her arm. The crown repeatedly slips off when she slumps sideways. Before she can remove the busily exploring snake, Foster must prop Cleopatra up and fix her crown. Finally, the throne bearing the queen proves too cumbersome to be carried up the centre aisle. Objects seem to be sabotaging action. . . .

At lunchtime, Muldowney rehearses the musicians in the auditorium. They are in costume, one or two incongruous in modern spectacles. Instruments and oddly-shaped cases clutter the aisles.

Cass Jones is up in the monument with a welding iron. The painting of the walls and of the 'stonework' surrounding the doors has been completed. Two men from the local fire department are in to do their usual pre-production check: they are concerned about whether the ramps into the aisles block the audience exit from the front of the stalls, and whether the flambeaux to be used in Antony's victory scene will be held above headdresses which could be flammable. Ernie Hall is able to reassure them on both counts.

In the afternoon, the cross-over from Pompey's galley to the scene in Parthia is re-run. Suddenly a section of the floor is violently torn up. The cue to fly out the rigging had been given whilst Hus Levent was still struggling, in the semi-darkness, to release the last hook attaching it to the stage. Immediately master carpenter Dennis Nolan is on the scene, hammering the projecting floor panel back into place.

The speed with which correctives take place, whenever there is a hitch, belies the surface calm of this last haul. Once again, Hall sits quietly in the darkened auditorium, trusting to the expertise of the production staff. At 5.00 p.m. a supper break is called and most of the actors rush to the canteen. Costumes are exchanged for dressing-gowns, but make-up, wigs and beards give the company an exotic group identity.

The Dress Rehearsal

The only opportunity to test the play right through, with synchronized effects, costume changes and daunting physical demands, before tomorrow's first public preview, the dress rehearsal starts (sharp) at 7.00 p.m. Having been off most of the previous evening and today, Hopkins is rested and immediately comfortable on this stage, with which he is so familiar. Judi Dench, still adjusting to the acoustics of the space, occasionally over-projects: it is astonishing how intimate a speech-level the multi-layered auditorium can take. The golden bull's-head mask worn by Mardian in the opening scene is knocked aside as Antony climbs off his shoulders. Michael Bryant looks like an old sea captain, in a full-whiskered beard. Visually, it makes a caricature of Enobarbus, contradicting any but his most obvious qualities.

John Haynes moves about in the front of the stalls, taking photos for 'front of house' (foyer) display, for distribution to the press and for the second run of programmes.

I am sitting next to a member of the Marketing Department who has not seen the play before. At the end of the first half, the possessive passion with which Caesar kisses his sister makes her nod vigorously: 'Oh, I see – it's incestuous.' When he hears about this reaction, Tim Pigott-Smith is delighted; what better proof could he have that he is making his obsession felt?

The evening is tense, hazardous. The mobile sections of the set collide several times. Andrew Wadsworth misses an entrance as Scarus, held up by a quick-change into ripped and blood-stained battledress. Then, during the capture of Cleopatra, when Patrick Brennan is scrambling over the iron gates into the monument, the gates are pulled apart too soon and a warning shout, 'Paddy's been hurt', stops the rehearsal.

It is an abrupt jolt back into the real world: Peter Hall rushes up onstage to where the actor lies in pain, a concerned group round him. Minutes pass. There is a hush in the auditorium. Finally, Brennan is supported offstage, limping, to be driven to St Thomas's Hospital nearby for an X-ray. Now that they are one supporting soldier short, the Dress Rehearsal picks up – on a subdued note – from after Cleopatra's descent.

After so many weeks, it suddenly feels, ridiculously, as if the play is under-rehearsed, the technical complications such as to require at least another week of integration. At 11.00 p.m., the cast disperses in low spirits. With a formidable mountain yet to be scaled, the adage 'bad dress rehearsal, good performance' is no comfort at all.

The following morning Hall is surprisingly encouraging: 'I wouldn't have minded if last night's rehearsal had been the first preview!

'We're now one and a half down: Simon Scott heard last night that his wife (expecting a baby) had gone into labour – so he's flown up to Scotland to be with her . . . and we'll have to do some covering for Patrick. Alan might have to go on.'

Cohen smiles bleakly. However Brennan, on crutches and in some pain from a badly torn ligament, is adamant about continuing: he has never yet missed a performance and is afraid that if he did so now, he 'might get to like it'.

'Last night the cry of "Where is my dresser?" was often heard,' continues Hall. 'There will be more working light backstage – and a catch on those doors.' (This is greeted with relief by the cast: the doors had frequently and irritatingly drifted open.) Dench asks that a torch and mirror be placed up in the monument. Hall requests that the actors wear dark clothing, if they are not rehearsing in costume, since Stephen Wentworth is still trying out lighting effects.

There are many individual problems to deal with: helmets that do not fit, beards to be reconsidered (David Schofield wears a small black goatee as Pompey, Michael Bryant's artificial whiskers are drastically reduced). Tony Hopkins and Jerry Flynn try out their 'suicide', using blood swords which pneumatically extrude a blood mixture from the point of the blade when the hilt is squeezed. (Blood bags carried under their shirts proved unreliable.) The wig department (also responsible for special make-up effects like wounds and scars) has constructed a latex mould for Des Adams' back. The Thidias scene is run: after being whipped, he is dragged back onstage, his shirt off. The simulated criss-cross of bloodied lines and torn flesh (glistening with Kyrolan – artificial blood) is horribly effective.

Judi Dench is feeling insecure, terrified by the height of the monument ('I'm so paralysed with fear up there that I don't know what comes out of me. . . .') and bothered about her shoes. Alison Chitty brings various pairs for her to try – about none of which is she completely happy: 'If only I could get out and buy something. I know exactly what I want. . . .'

Yet, in the midst of anxiety, her focus is unswerving: is there anything, she wonders, that was uncovered during rehearsals which she may have since forgotten? 'Only the birth of Cleopatra's twins,' I tease. In her black velvet tracksuit and boots, her blonde hair catching the light, she looks slight and vulnerable against the great circle of the darkened stage.

Sally Dexter is in low mood, unusual for her: 'Octavia is on and off so quickly that I can't tell if it's working. . . .' The technical week can be alienating: as they developed their characters, the actors had depended on a confirmation (from Hall and their fellow-actors) which is no longer there. In the gloomy aftermath of the dress rehearsal, and as they begin to gear themselves up for public exposure, there is a sudden, almost panicky hunger for last-minute feedback – irrespective of source. John Bluthal glows at hearing that Lepidus has the 'presence' he has been striving for. Helen Fitzgerald wants to be assured that Iras and Charmian are distinct personalities. Des Adams gives a gentle smile of relief that Thidias' seductive gallantry towards Cleopatra, recently heightened, is now obvious.

Basil Henson rather throws me when he enquires whether I have noticed he has been making Agrippa increasingly critical of Caesar. Well, yes, I have noticed a mounting strain, a pointed hesitation in his responses to his leader. When, for example, Caesar commands: 'Our will is Antony be took alive', Henson glares at him with undisguised contempt – and he has finally persuaded Peter Hall that he should *not* be onstage for the final scene in the play, that of Caesar's triumph. But isn't Henson's approach somewhat perverse, I ask? After all, Agrippa gave lifelong service to Caesar. . . .

However, I am being obtuse. I begin to see that the actor's reconsidered approach is dramatically intriguing. And he will soon prove it viable, when John Peter writes in the *Sunday Times*: '[Caesar's] dishonesties are not lost on his followers, especially Basil Henson's fastidious Agrippa', and an American critic, Alan Dessen, endorses 'a statesmanlike, well-defined Agrippa . . . distancing himself (as a Roman loyal to something larger than one individual) from Octavius' vengeful choices'. Justifying Henson's interpretation at points throughout the text, Dessen concludes: 'For the first time I understood why Dolabella, Proculeius and others, but not Agrippa, are central to the final sequence with Cleopatra.' Case well fought, Henson!

By contrast with the actors' need for reassurance, those out front are markedly confident. Julia Wilson-Dixon claims that she has never seen the Olivier better used in terms of set: it truly contains the actors, assists them to project language and performance. At the end of twenty minutes of last night's dress rehearsal, she had made no notes; at the end of fifty minutes, only three, and she then settled down to enjoy the play. Hall's approach has imposed absolute clarity on the text, and then given the actors the freedom to use it as a real springboard to emotion and character.

Hall himself sits chatting to a group of actors at the front of the stalls. Relaxed and good-humoured, he is enjoying this stage of the proceedings. He and Jerry Flynn mull over the idea that Shakespeare would have been writing for the cinema, had he been alive today. . . . Hall's thoughts freewheel: during the dress rehearsal, the smoke from the funeral pyre in the Parthian scene, and that pumped over the stage during the sea-battle, had continued to hang over the scenes which followed. In passing, the director relishes an image of the entire play done with smoke drifting across it. . . .

Malcolm Ranson and Alan Cohen rework the siege on the monument which caused last night's injury. Two horizontal poles are used to raise Cleopatra's throne, but this proves insecure. Ranson now orchestrates an exit whereby Judi Dench is lifted on to the shoulders of six soldiers and carried up the centre aisle, in step with Muldowney's funeral march. Enfolded in her gold robes, arms across her breast, Dench is an image from the Egypt of the Pharaohs.

Before the rehearsal breaks, the cast assemble to work out a curtain call. Hall is deliberately casual: 'I like it fairly rough for previews, nothing too formal.' Judi Dench: 'As though you'd never got round to organizing it. . . .' From all points of the auditorium and wings the actors make for the stage, there to spread loosely round Cleopatra, Antony, Caesar and Enobarbus, taking the cue for the bows from them.

Cleaners descend upon the Olivier, to clear the day's debris: half-finished cups of coffee, paper plates, buckets serving as ashtrays, forgotten sweaters. Lighting, console and director's desk are removed from the stalls. The stage staff are busy with last-minute adjustments: the cyclorama – which had been hanging in shadowy folds – is stretched flat and the central cut-out, into which the doors recede, attached to a backing frame. Floor panels are double-checked for signs of buckling. After a quick supper, stage management are back at their posts: all the props have been re-set and Emma Lloyd does a final survey, as the stage is being swept. Paul Greaves retires to the right-hand vomitory from where he will prompt.

Arditti does a last check on sound. Stephen Wentworth runs through lighting cues on the computer in the control box; the doors and walls onstage, winched to their pre-set positions, are lit to await the entrance of the audience.

Marney Meakin, House Manager of the Olivier, lectures her team of ushers about the particular demands of this production: manning the doors, they must anticipate the numerous entrances and exits through the aisles, and protect unsuspecting members of the audience from charging hordes of thespians. There is a routine fire drill, the ushers go to their posts and, after conferring with Angie Bissett (who relays 'the house is now open' to Ernie Hall backstage) Ms Meakin gives the signal to open the doors to the foyer.

CHAPTER 11

Previews – Learning from an Audience Presence

WEEK 12/13 – Friday 3 April to Wednesday 8 April

From the time when priority booking opened in mid-January, tickets for *Antony and Cleopatra* went rapidly. Now, all performances, including previews, are sold out until the end of May, when the next booking period begins. There were people queuing for the forty day seats from nine o'clock in the morning. The combination of Shakespeare, Hall, Dench and Hopkins makes excellent box office.

Nevertheless, after twelve weeks under wraps, it is quite startling to come to terms with the actuality: an audience of over a thousand people swarming into the auditorium, filling it with colour and the buzz of anticipation. The back row of the stalls is reserved for members of the production team: what marks them out from the public is that there is not a single programme between the lot of them – no one has collected a free copy backstage and no one is paying 80p to acquire one!

Hall sits in the glass-fronted director's box rear stalls, Alan Cohen beside him to take notes.

Although the opening sequence is uneasy – could the audience be taken aback by the sexual rough-and-tumble between Dench and Hopkins? – at their next entrance, these two take command. Many of Dench's perverse lines and capricious swirls get laughter: she responds with added bite. Hopkins gives the language more weight; sensing attentiveness, he locks in to each moment, adding but also leaving out gestures which one had come to anticipate in rehearsal, if they no longer ring true. Likewise heightened, Pigott-Smith's performance makes Caesar awkward and ill-at-ease, as he sits twisting one ankle behind the other, picking petulantly at the arm of his chair.

Stephen Wentworth has said that lighting should be part of the total emotional impact, never noticeable, and indeed I have to make a conscious effort to watch for it. An interesting dappled effect, seeming to suggest Antony's ambivalence, covers the stage for the first meeting between him and Octavia, and sets it up for the ominous appearance of the Soothsayer.

David Schofield revels in the audience presence, savouring, almost tasting the language. At the end of the galley scene, he leaps off the table at Hopkins ('Antony, you have my father's house'), instead of waiting for the latter to pull him down, a move so expressive of the anger in the line that one can only wonder that it did not occur to him sooner. As they exit down the ramp into the centre aisle, Schofield intuitively recoils from the friendly hand which Antony is about to place on his shoulder: also splendid moment-to-moment stuff.

Bryant's description of Cleopatra at Cydnus, as fresh-minted as ever, gets a burst of spontaneous applause, as does Dench's virago-like attack on the Messenger.

Despite a few technical hitches – a missed entrance, a wall section which does not move in on a scene – Part One of the play has enormous pace and vitality, reflected in the audience's animated chatter at the interval.

In Part Two, after the defeat of Actium, Antony falls face-down on the floor in shame, and Cleopatra keens with grief. 'Let's have one other gaudy night' is a brave flag waved against declining fortune, a resurgence of their charismatic zest for life.

From then on, however, Hopkins pursues a line of despair, his legs giving way so that he becomes almost aged in defeat. He emerges for the second day of battle not rejuvenated, but already haunted by failure. The mood grows doom-laden, its pervasive pessimism tiring the audience when they should be moved. As a result, the mechanics of the play are thrown into negative perspective: suddenly there appear to be too many exits and entrances through the aisles, the three-days-of-battle loses definition and when Antony is hauled up to the monument, there is laughter from the audience. In this atmosphere, his death takes on the feel of melodrama and it is a struggle to recapture the sympathetic attention of the house.

As the audience leaves, the only comments I hear refer to the extreme length of the play.

Backstage, the actors are slightly dazed: although for Paddy Brennan there is personal triumph in having hobbled through his scenes on crutches (even managing to make it look like a piece of staged realism), all of them were too busy with costume changes and getting to the right entrance on time, to be able to assess overall audience reaction – or to be aware of the turgid pace of Part Two.

Previews are an excellent testing ground: the presence of an audience throws into relief the strong or weak patches in a production, and there is an opportunity to make adjustments at rehearsals in between.

On the morning after the first preview, Hall's left eye is inflamed with conjunctivitis. Somewhat wanly, he jokes about being very protective of this one, ever since he lost most of the sight in the other. Given his keen pictorial sense, this is a revelation.

Again, he is surprisingly calm, his confidence in production and cast apparently unshaken: 'It packs a punch. I was really thrilled with what was going on last night, knowing that it works, it holds, unfolds and is exciting. That's unusually good for a play of this size. You have the extreme formal discipline needed – what does it mean: what is the shape of the verse? where is it going? – so take it, and scare the shit out of them!

'This play has such a vast span of contrasts, a symphonic complexity, that the danger is that you will not endorse it. Look at the reversals: a woman goes to war (she shouldn't), Antony is never beaten (he is), he is confident, a winner (he breaks down), he is adorable and to be followed (he becomes disgusting), they are the greatest lovers in the world (a rift comes between them), he engenders loyalty (he is deserted), he will lose (he wins), he will win (he loses), he will die heroically (he dies like a stuck pig), she is opportunistic (she is loyal and dies with courage). You know the story; don't anticipate it, but take each movement as it comes.

'The whole of this world is up for grabs, it's about greed and gambling.' This leads into a note for Hopkins: 'Antony is a gambler with life for whom things have always turned out well. Even in marriage to Octavia, he believes he can have his cake and eat it. Enjoy it, Tony! The obverse side is his paranoia when things begin to go wrong. Antony always surprises the audience by not doing or being what they expect: it's a roller-coaster effect.' He seems to be telling the actor to ride with each switch of Antony's emotional state, rather than pursue a single course with such tenacity.

Delighted with the first half of the play, the director found the second 'choppy' and blames himself: he needs to tighten the marching and the lighting cues considerably. . . .

Various cast members are not sure whether to speak as they come on, before the lights are fully up. Hall assures them that the issue will not arise (saying, in an aside to Wentworth: 'That old technique that we use, dipping to a back light and then building the scene up, won't do here'). The brevity of scenes dictates that the mood – and a full state of lighting – must be established at the outset of each.

Ranson drills a phalanx of soldiers crossing the stage, going over and over it, until they're all marching in step. Since they emerge from a tight space in the wings, those at the back have to mark time whilst the front ranks lead off. The night before there had been quite a lot of scuttling to close ranks which, viewed out front, was distinctly comical. Hall stands by until they achieve the uniform trudging rhythm that he wants.

Later, he wants to simplify the sequence in which Antony's band runs through the auditorium in pursuit of Agrippa and his soldiers. Hopkins, undaunted by the amount of distance that has to be covered, is keen that it be kept in: 'It gets the adrenalin going!' Hall concedes, smiling at the actor's energy. What had been something of a scramble at the preview is now broken down into stages, so that the manoeuvres of the opposing sides emerge with absolute clarity.

As they go over other scenes, he alters actors' positions on the stage ('to deepen the picture') and changes points of entry to speed up the overlap of scenes. Tony Hopkins and John Bluthal are late on a newly-staged entrance: 'The Triumvirs one has to work with,' sighs Tim Pigott-Smith in mock despair.

It was during the second preview that a practical crisis occurred which opened the door to a deeper problem.

As Hopkins rose to the monument, the rope jammed and he hung there whilst those at the top hauled away fruitlessly. Finally, inch by inch, they managed to get him up on to the balcony but by then the audience (many of them laughing) were disengaged – and remained so until the end of the play.

The ascent obviously needed to be rethought: on successive nights, it had had an element of the ridiculous, caused perhaps by Antony's active participation when he is supposed to be in his death throes. Hall and his designer discussed an alternative: a large rope net would cradle a seemingly helpless Antony and carry him aloft. The props department would be mobilized to construct the net during Sunday, ready for use at Monday's rehearsal.

When Hall telephoned Dench to tell her about the improvement it emerged that she had been growing more and more depressed throughout the production week. She felt that the play had lost direction and that she was 'on a choppy sea, unsure of the voyage being taken'.

She put her finger on it when she said that the feeling between Antony and Cleopatra had gone. Without the central love, the romantic passion, we do not care about them, and all the peripheral action becomes meaningless.

Dench was speaking from a honed intuitive sense, but, of course, if one analyses the chemistry between onlooker and performer, a mechanical hiccup should not have destroyed attention to the extent that it did. An emotionally involved audience would have wanted to preserve, or to be led back to, the necessary state of 'suspended disbelief'.

Hall decided that he, Dench and Hopkins should get together in a session on the Monday morning: the intention – to rediscover the premise on which *Antony and Cleopatra* rests.

Accordingly, on Monday the rest of the cast were not called until the afternoon, whilst Hall returned to the rehearsal room with his two leading actors.

That evening, I watch Part One of the play from the wings stage left, near the traditional prompt corner, Ernie Hall's tannoying point. He and Emma Lloyd are in headsets, transmitters at their waists. The funeral bier for the Parthian scene is standing by, halberds are propped against a fixed central column (enclosing the counter-weights for the manual flying of scenery) and space is surprisingly limited. All backstage personnel wear black clothes and rubber-soled shoes.

Stage manager Ernie Hall gives the half-hour call, the fifteen minutes, the five, and then summons the actors involved in the opening scene: 'Act I, beginners onstage, please: Mr Hayward, Mr Spink, Miss Dench, Mr Hopkins, Miss Foster. . . .' It is curiously Edwardian ('Miss Terry, Mr Tree, Mrs Campbell, Mr Forbes Robertson. . . .'). Actors start to gather. Father of a newborn son,

Simon Scott is back from Scotland: as tonight is his first performance he is nervous, not least about whether he has been fully briefed about changes during his absence. Ernie Hall watches the action on a monitor screen and, once the play has started, summons Thorndike and Bryant for the following scene. The stage itself feels a great distance away. As Dench and Hopkins come off, their dressers, Lou and Gilly, swoop in to escort them back to their dressing-rooms for a quick change. Ernie Hall gives the winch-operator on the centre doors a standby for the next cue 'only because he didn't seem to be there': when Angie Bissett 'flashed' him, he had not responded. The operator acknowledges this failsafe standby, and the doors move back on cue. Now a call goes out to the actors in the first Caesar/Lepidus scene and Props get a standby for the chairs, which they prepare to hand over to the three young actors who will carry them on stage.

Dressers come in and out through the swing doors leading to the dressing-rooms, removing helmets, bringing back cloaks. Having delivered his first lines, Simon Scott feels more confident. Waiting actors sit on the steps beyond the stage 'Exit' sign, smoking and chatting.

'Lights down, Part One', alerts everyone backstage to the coming Interval. Once it starts, Ernie Hall makes a courtesy call to Anthony Hopkins, to give him the running time of the first half (on which the actor likes to keep tabs). The shutters go up on the scene-dock and props no longer to be used are cleared away. Winches, the monument mechanism and props for the second half are checked. In preparation for entrances down the aisles, drums, banners and shields are carried round to the front-of-house. Everyone is still feeling their way into what will become routine. Mike Hayward prowls the wings, anxious about the end of the play: after Cleopatra's death, the garter snake goes back into its basket – which he has to open. . . .

I watch the rest of the play from the stalls. It is remarkably transformed. Hopkins has pulled back from his bravado and emotionalism into a figure of sober dignity, cracking only at the edges.

This radically alters the colouring of each scene: in the attack on Thidias, he is no longer rolling drunk but deeply hurt by Cleopatra's apparent betrayal. The reconciliation between them is passionate and warm. When the servants are called in, a deep inward grief has replaced the wild self-pity: Antony seems to have realized that he is responsible for his downfall and, if his mind is disturbed, his actions are composed. The magnanimity and fortitude of the character rise to the surface – and we are moved by the tragedy of his decline, now that he is no longer raging against it blindly.

Above all, the axis of the play has been restored. Dench is no longer fighting for Hopkins' attention but has it wholly. When she dresses him in his armour, there is great tenderness between them, an echo of their former playfulness. Their passion may have brought them to the brink of destruction, but, as long as it holds – and we see evidence of its endurance – the rewards of the external world seem petty and well-lost by comparison.

One scene breaks upon another, almost like a series of waves. For the first time, I believe I understand what Peter Hall meant by 'endorsing' the play, an attitude he has urged on several occasions – without explanation: the actors are open to the emotional currents in each scene, giving each an innate logic and richness.

The audience, caught up in the unfolding drama, is absolutely still and attentive, expectation challenged by every reversal of fortune and mood, appetite sharpened for what is to follow.

Not surprisingly, tonight when Antony is hauled up to the monument in the net, there is not a sound. Dench moves from a savage despair at his death to an almost ecstatic state as she anticipates her own. I remember that Peter Hall, in a newspaper interview, had called her 'the pre-eminent actress – the greatest speaker of Shakespeare in her generation'. After she is borne up the aisle and the lights come down, there are several seconds of silence, before tumultuous applause fills the auditorium and breaks the spell. What we had seen tonight was unquestionably a love story.

Explaining the change, Hopkins is disarmingly self-deprecating: 'I'd been playing it like Godzilla, shutting Judi out. Now we're going for the love, the communication between them. It's amazing that one has to go through so much just to get back to the original, simple concepts.

'By playing Antony larger than life, pumping out energy and approaching the whole thing as an extrovert, I'd got far away from my inner emotions. I remember when I first met Olivier, he did ordinary things, looked ordinary – like a bank manager, hair thinning, quietly spoken, conservative suit – yet he exuded this enormous energy. I'd made Antony strut – the really great spirits don't.

'Peter challenged the drunkenness: "It's exciting, but does it help the relationship between you?" I told him that I couldn't be maudlin without it, so he let me give up that self-pity and play it as though Antony is aware that he's finished, that it's been of his own making, and that all he can do is go along with it.'

On Tuesday morning, 7 April, with only two days to go before 'lift off', changes are still being made. Today the Parthian scene is augmented: seven more soldiers are drafted in. (Peter Hall: 'It's so much more potent if it looks like a real army.' Muttering from veterans in the darkened auditorium: 'Less is more. . . . ') The casting department has rounded up actors who are already on the NT payroll, but would be free for performances of *Antony and Cleopatra*: one turns up to rehearse in a high collar and tails, in a break from a matinee of *The Magistrate*. Chitty and the wardrobe team are (in her words) 'working a not inconsiderable miracle' assembling appropriate dress for them, some of it recycled from *Coriolanus*. And the body of Pacorus, the king's son (a lolling Simon Needs) is now to be carried in and tossed on the floor, before being displayed in the bier. It is a detail, but the callousness of the gesture clinches the scene. These are barbarous times.

When they go on to a scene-by-scene 'topping and tailing', running just the overlaps between them to speed up the cues, Alan Cohen does most of the legwork and vocalizing, chasing up the centre aisle to discuss an improvement with the director, bouncing up on to the stage to sort out a problem. 'If you're carrying a banner, hold it up high for a good, strong image,' he says, and demonstrates how by bracing the pole of a banner against his diaphragm.

For the *n*th – and final – time, Hall challenges the actors' reluctance to come in on a new scene whilst those in the previous scene are still delivering their final lines: 'It's an actor's instinct to be courteous to his colleagues – and to protect his own interests.' (This raises a knowing laugh: on making an entrance, who wants to share the audience's attention?) 'But,' continues Hall, 'it's not Shakespearean to come on to a soft, low-temperatured stage. It should be like marvellous strong film cutting.'

When the scene on Pompey's galley is run (for the benefit of the musicians and young singers), Hall asks that by the time Caesar complains 'Let me request you off', he and Antony be no longer entangled on the floor. 'You purist, Peter,' smiles Tim Pigott-Smith. 'Oh, only until I've gone,' returns Hall. 'Then you can do as you like!'

Not so. The production will be closely monitored by Ernie Hall and Alan Cohen, so that it stays true to Hall's concept and detail. NT management will receive the stage manager's report on every performance and, to keep vitality pumping through the work, Hall will himself drop in on performances and periodically take word-runs.

On the evidence of the third preview, and as a result of the last few days' work, the whole play is considerably tighter. Because of their added manpower and Ranson's painstaking drilling, the group sequences are now paying off: in visual and emotional terms, these co-ordinated phalanxes of soldiers add a weighty pomp and aggression to the Roman scenes. At other times, charging in behind the colours of Caesar or Antony, they palpably embody the military power each wields – especially once the numbers begin to peel away from Antony and swell the ranks of Caesar.

The fact that the play pivots on the relationship between Cleopatra and Antony, its romantic quality, continues to build. The Egyptian scenes are suffused with sexual tension. As well as the former flamboyance of their passion, there is a more intimate communication – which reaches the audience. When they are separated, Dench and Hopkins evoke a yearning for each other which creates a dramatic pressure for them to be reunited. In Part Two, there is a desperation to maintain the bond whilst their worldly power crumbles: with his death she races towards her own: 'quick – methinks I hear Antony call'.

The following morning Hall is delighted: 'So many of the things which have never been achieved before, happened last night.' By now the actors can anticipate his comments on their performances: either they got something wrong and know it, or they have clear reasons for the choices they made.

After lunch there is a photo-call for a number of freelancers and the press (who like to do their own coverage, although their picture editors will have received a selection of John Haynes' photographs). Nicki Frei circulates amongst them. To save valuable time, she and the production team have chosen specific scenes for the call. The actors assemble in costume and make-up and the session is briskly dealt with, as a semi-circle of cameras click away in the stalls.

The staff photographer from *The Independent* lingers to take pictures of Peter Hall who, somewhat self-consciously, puts on his black leather jacket, combs his hair and goes up on to the stage to subject the central doors of the set to a close – and unnecessary – scrutiny.

The doors at the back of the stalls and circle are being rehung and oiled: as early as November 1975 Hall had started to ask that the doors in the then new theatre be fixed: 'the front-of-house doors didn't fit and . . . the automatic closing devices made them squeak'. That it has taken almost twelve years for his complaints to be heeded is an irony he remarks on. A rearguard battle finally won.

And talking of battles, Iain Ormsby-Knox, as Equity deputy (a position for which he volunteered early in rehearsals), raises an issue caused by the unusual length of the play: there will be only a one-hour break between the matinée and evening show on those days when the play is performed twice. Since a two-hour break is statutory, there is a demand by some of the company for overtime pay, although most of the veterans of the company are used to the situation. 'That's life,' says Michael Bryant, 'but the young Turks want a change.'

Ormsby-Knox has a personal dilemma: on behalf of the company, he is having to negotiate with the casting department – on whom his future at the National depends. Thus far, they are proving intransigent. Were the issue to harden, he could be dubbed a troublemaker. At the end of the afternoon he is embroiled in discussion in Gillian Diamond's office – and not looking happy. Later still, he praises Hall's stance: the latter has offered to intercede between actors and management, so that Ormsby-Knox does not have to take all the onus on himself. The 'compromise' reached is a 1.30 p.m. start for matinées, allowing for a 1½-hour turnaround before the evening show. No overtime was paid for the extra half-hour to which the actors were entitled.

Wanting to clear my head for tomorrow's official opening night, I watch the first few scenes of the final preview, and then go off to see a comedy act in Soho.

CHAPTER 12

The Press Night – 'Judgements Made at a Gambling Moment'

When *Antony and Cleopatra* first went into rehearsal, it was the middle of winter. Thursday 9 April is a perfect spring day, with light sparkling off the river and skies of clear blue. In the theatre foyers there is a smell of fresh polish.

Judi Dench and a cluster of other actors are sitting in the canteen. Some have slept soundly the night before. Dench has not. If the task ahead is something of an ordeal, her humour is intact. Miranda Foster is cheerful. Despite a lot of anxiety about achieving what Hall wanted during rehearsals, she is now enjoying performances. Her parents will be at tonight's. (Since she does not resemble him in voice, looks or movement, it is a surprise to learn that her father is the actor Barry Foster.) Blanketing excitement and nerves, conversation tends to be deliberately mundane.

At the stage door, a poster of the play and mounting piles of good luck cards await each actor, every pile topped by a pyramid-shaped chocolate bar from Judi Dench. Flowers arrive for her throughout the day. On a board near the Olivier stage is a giant card from tonight's boy singer, Peter Corey, good wishes to the newly-recruited 'soldiers' from Dench – and Daniel Thorndike's 'Personal Sonnetal Sooth':

> It shall be yet far longer than you thought
> Yet new recruits arrive each minute some . . .
> Isis help! Emm says my banner's wrong!
> You may escape the critics' Parthian dart
> But if indulgent pauses get too long
> Yer end will be o'ertaken by yer start.
> We're all encased by blood red walls and Cyc
> So loving friends our fortunes are alike!

Stephen Wentworth is making final adjustments to the lighting. He has never lit a show with as many cues: where big productions normally have about 120, *Antony and Cleopatra* has almost 170. Having started as an electrician at the Old Vic fourteen years before, Wentworth is still contracted to the National on that basis. Combined with his involvement as a resident Lighting Designer, it gives him 'a good combination of security, getting my hands dirty and creative opportunities'. After tonight (which he will oversee from the lighting box), he will work as one of the smoke operators on the show.

With the speed demanded on this production, Wentworth feels that his design vision is being compromised, but then 'I consider giving up as a designer after each show, I am so filled with anguish about it'. (In fact, his lighting is becoming increasingly evocative. Frequently the protagonists are strongly illuminated, surrounded by pools of darkness. This mirrors the emotion in a scene which, depending on circumstance, can be a comfortable intimacy, a haunting sense of isolation and loss, or a sharp signal of dramatic reversal.) The designer speaks highly of Hall's spatial sense and his strength at 'telling the story'.

On the stage itself, selected scenes are run for lighting cues. Dench is in her tracksuit, Tony Hopkins in the dark suit and tie he will be wearing for tonight's reception after the show. He is playful, seemingly without a care. The actors are conserving energy, not projecting their lines, there are few people in the auditorium and, for a brief period, it is like being back in the rehearsal room again.

Andrew Wadsworth is watching from the stalls. This production has been difficult for him: he is not particularly happy with his parts and now he feels that the various departments – wardrobe and wigs – are treating him according to his 'weight' in the play, rather than with the loyalty due to someone they have known for two years. On the positive side, his rewards have been watching Hall and Hopkins work: 'I love Tony for his risk-taking and experimentation. I'm sorry that the drunkenness and buckling knees have gone. And I've never seen Peter so fired. . . .'

The cast gather for a final 'team talk' from the director, preceded by a caution: 'It's starting to spread – and it's not the indulgence of the leaders of the world, but the indulgence of actors!

'In tonight's audience, you won't only have the critics, but also people who feel they've paid for the show (the Ladbrokes sponsors). They could be hostile or cold. My advice to you is – don't harangue them or shout. Make them come to you. I know we've got something good – and so do you.'

Earlier that day, referring to critical appraisal, Hall had said to me that one of the hard things about theatre is that 'judgements are made at a gambling moment'. Historically these judgements mattered, he supposed – although, as with *Waiting for Godot* in 1955, and the David Warner *Hamlet* in 1965, he had done some famous productions 'which got terrible reviews, really terrible – and then took on a mythical status'. He cared about criticism insofar as it could stop people coming to see a play, or 'if it discourages the actors so that growth doesn't go on'.

Now he says to them: 'What really interests me is what this production will be like in three months' time, when you've really got into it and the blood is flowing. It's already full and rich, and when you've bedded down, I think it will be extraordinary.' Urging his cast to 'think forward to that', he is assuring them, in no uncertain terms, of the quality of their work over the past three months. The judgement of the critics is to be kept in perspective.

'I must tell you that I've never enjoyed anything more in my whole life, and I wish it wasn't over,' he says. After that, curtain calls are carefully timed and orchestrated: related groups enter, followed by the individual leads. Then, with no great formality, the actors disappear to their dressing-rooms or the canteen: Hall will go round giving good wishes and personal thanks to them all.

Anthony Hopkins' dressing-room is like a crowded bedsit, divided into shower compartment, a section with hand basin and make-up table, and a bed and armchair by the window. The walls are papered with cards, mostly mystical – Pre-Raphaelite and Celtic. Plants on the window-sill filter the light. Still in his suit, sitting in the armchair, Hopkins is chuckling over first-night cards and letters.

He exudes energy and warmth: 'This is the most extraordinary production I've ever been in: Peter makes you feel anything is possible. When I saw the set, designs and costumes I sensed it was going to be interesting. Then I had that period when I felt "God, no – I can't do it". But now . . . I feel calm and can't wait to get out there. And it's all the amazing vision of one man. . . .'

At 5.30 p.m. I go through one of the doors leading from the backstage area to the front-of-house. Tonight's performance will start at 6.45 p.m., to allow an earlier getaway for the critics, who have complimentary tickets (in many cases for their 'regular' seats on the aisles in the stalls). Only 143 pairs of 'comps' have been issued for the first and second nights, to include those for staff. Mindful of income from tickets that are sold, the NT is tight-fisted with its allocation of free ones.

The foyers are starting to fill. A steady flow of *Antony and Cleopatra* actors and production staff make their way to the book-shop for last-minute cards. Music Manager Kevin Leeman is one of them. (Dominic Muldowney, who avoids press nights, has done his usual disappearance to France, leaving Leeman in charge.)

At the stalls level of the Olivier, Ladbrokes have installed a 'hospitality marquee', providing a panoramic view of the river and champagne and canapés for their guests (amongst whom is the Home Secretary, Douglas Hurd, also responsible for the gaming laws of the country). Cyril Stein, Ladbrokes' chairman, circulates. There is a smattering of NT personnel – John Faulkner, Head of Artistic Planning, Josette Nicholls, responsible for the 'marriage' between sponsors and theatre, and Thelma Holt, Head of Touring and Commercial Exploitation (who had set up the *Antony and Cleopatra* trips to Greece and Egypt – now unfortunately cancelled).

The critics start to arrive: Irving Wardle of *The Times*, Milton Shulman of the *Standard*, the *Guardian*'s Michael Billington. Amongst those collecting their programmes from the Press Desk in the foyer are several radio reviewers: Martin Appleby of the BBC's 'First Night' will go out live, with his opinion of the production, ten minutes after this evening's performance ends.

It is very much a well-heeled 'first night' audience which starts to filter into the auditorium, more typical of the West End than the National, where one is usually part of a colourful cross-section of the theatregoing public. Peter Hall, an interested onlooker, is leaning nonchalantly against the wall at the head of the stalls. This is his patch, his working home, and I wonder how it must feel to watch it fill up, and know that three months of creative input is about to be assessed. Angie Bissett tannoys stragglers in the foyer to make for their seats: 'The performance will begin in three minutes, ladies and gentlemen, three minutes please. . . .'

Facing them, the set is monumentally impressive and rich-toned, the interlocked curve of doors and walls sculptural against the dark background.

Precisely on time, the performance begins: the houselights fall, the cosmic drone fills the air, the audience stills and the doors are thrust apart.

Mike Hayward and Brian Spink deliver the play's opening lines with assurance and deliberation. Then the Egyptian court bursts in, and the stage is filled with a sinuous jangle of music, hot colour and action. Immediately the quality of the central relationship is established: the public display, the deep intimacy beneath.

Forgetting the notebook and pen in my lap, I am engulfed and swept forward by the global narrative, along with the rest of the audience. They are self-conscious, not easy to play to, yet from the first the production demands their attention – and keeps a tenacious hold upon it. Cleopatra's energetic attack on the Messenger releases waves of unexpected laughter.

Performance by the entire cast is deftly placed, absolutely intelligent and intelligible. The story has never been better told. Nothing uncovered in rehearsals is neglected or skimmed.

Behind their performances, I see shadows of the actors' own personae: Sally Dexter exuberant and beaming, in an over-sized denim jacket, David Schofield adjusting black-rimmed spectacles as he practises a complex tap-routine, Hus Levent demonstrating the steps of a Turkish dance. . . . As Graham Sinclair strokes the folds of his velvet cloak, a poised and self-aware Maecenas, I remember him in sweater and jeans, directing a platform performance. As John Bluthal offers the basket of figs to Judi Dench, loading each of his lines with *double entendre*, I think of him puffing at a cigar, contemplating the rich potential of the Clown. . . .

The performance ends on a high, noble note and is greeted with a standing ovation, extended applause and cheers. There can be no regrets that the detail and dramatic power of this production has been less than masterfully conveyed.

Afterwards, Ladbrokes hold a first-night party on the Olivier stage: groundsheets protect the floor of the set, buffet tables are laid out and white-gloved waiters hand round drinks and food. There is a slight feeling of oil and water between the company of *Antony and Cleopatra* and the other guests. Josette Nicholls does an excellent line in introductions, but the former show a marked tendency to cling together: because performances end so late, this is the first 'aftermath' they are able to share. Having circulated, Peter Hall, too, ends up surrounded by members of the production team and actors.

The cast are exhilarated, running off the adrenalin built up through the evening. At one point during the play, Judi Dench had crashed into a wall-section as she rushed off the darkened stage. Relieved that this was the only mishap, she shrugs off the swollen lip which is the result: 'I've never before experienced a first night when my nerves were entirely taken up with problems. Either I was busy preparing to haul Tony up, or leap from the monument, or deal with the snake. . . . It was wonderfully focusing!'

This is the euphoric hiatus between having delivered and awaiting the verdict. The mood is emotional; aware that the daily camaraderie of rehearsals is at an end, and despite two performances the next day, nobody wants to go home.

No matter the excellence of its ingredients, the chemistry of a piece of theatre is unpredictable. Even if it seems to be working during rehearsal, there is no guarantee that the public will agree. And even if the public agrees and the chemistry works for most performances, on some nights, Press Night included, it may misfire.

The importance of the reviews had been deliberately underplayed by Hall. My own focus was the exploration of rehearsals: I had wanted to cover *Antony and Cleopatra* because its component parts, and the process by which they were integrated, promised to be of intrinsic value, regardless of critical reception.

Nevertheless, everyone involved cannot help being keenly interested as the first notices start to appear. Hall's 'judgements made at a gambling moment' assume an almost roulette-wheel fascination – and the rest, as they say, is history. . . .

RENAISSANCE OF THE GOLDEN AGE – *Sunday Times*
THE ULTIMATE ROMANCE – *Guardian*
ELECTRIFYING DETAIL AND TRAGIC
EXHILARATION – *The Times*
TRIUMPH IN DEATH ON THE NILE – *Observer*

'This is easily the most satisfying *Antony and Cleopatra* I have ever seen,' avows Michael Coveney in the *Financial Times* of Friday 10

April. Neither has Charles Osborne (*Daily Telegraph*) ever seen 'a more exciting and satisfying production of the play . . . one does not have to peer through the intellectual fog of directors' "interpretation" to discern Shakespeare's creation, and at no point is sound sacrificed [to] sense'. He lauds 'an unobtrusive but commanding intelligence which sets the play before the audience with utmost clarity'.

The day before he reviewed *Antony and Cleopatra*, Michael Billington had raised the question of Shakespearean acting in Britain, with his readers in the *Guardian*. Like Hall, he perceived a growing crisis: due to the dearth of appropriate acting opportunities and 'a decline in verbal culture, actors are losing the ability to relish Shakespeare's irony, ambiguity and play of imagery *which was a cardinal feature of Peter Hall's policy in creating the RSC* [my italics] . . . to handle Shakespeare's language with a witty, confident intelligence that used to be the RSC hallmark'.

He sees 'no hint of crisis' in Hall's new production, however. It is 'the most intelligently-spoken Shakespeare I have seen in years'. Judi Dench's 'breathtaking Cleopatra' and Anthony Hopkins' 'magnificent Antony' he ranks (as do several other reviewers) with those of Ashcroft and Redgrave, thirty-five years before, bypassing interpretations in the interim years.

For Billington: 'Like all great Shakespearean productions, Peter Hall's uncovers meanings in the text that may seem obvious but that have never hit one so penetratingly before'. For Coveney: 'The panoply of war is . . . coolly presented with a great variety of staging manoeuvres and a great patience with nooks and crannies one had hardly noticed before' (such as the Ventidius scene in Parthia). He also notes that 'Women have a rough time of it in the soldiers' world'. The play's concern with public image and prestige – as underlined by Hall – is picked up by the *Independent*'s Peter Kemp.

Steve Grant of the influential 'alternative' magazine *Time Out*, homes in on 'Maturity . . . the keynote of this stunning evening. A mature play, starring two mature players ably supported by . . . Michael Bryant's peerless Enobarbus'. The production by Peter Hall is 'lucid, expertly paced, gimmick-free and though occasionally over-robust in its full use of the auditorium (someone's gonna get speared one night, mark me) always in control of a text that coils, spits and bursts. . . .'

Other critics refer to Hall's 'masterful' use of the Olivier, stage and auditorium, and the 'cinematic fluidity' of his direction.

John Peter's review in the *Sunday Times* (his is the headline 'Renaissance of the Golden Age') resounds with recognition: 'Golden ages of the theatre are usually in the past – but we may be living in one today. Peter Hall's production . . . is *the British theatre at its spellbinding and magnificent best* (my italics). This is a big, heroic play in every sense, and Hall's control over it is complete. The huge spans of the action tense up, arch and unfold like great symphonic movements, and the poetry of this sensuous, athletic text tolls with burnished conviction. Hall reminds us, and we do need reminding, that the bedrock of classical theatre is the text; that the life of the play is first and most essentially in the words of the play, and that visual splendour and the excitement of action needs to be justified by a sense that the words are both felt and understood. Without that, we have theatricality, which is like inflation. Hall deals in sound currency. This is the real thing.

'Anthony Hopkins and Judi Dench play the title roles as if they were not star actors. There is a moving and painful honesty in these performances: they are fleshy, ageing people, both of them attractive and difficult, and they give a sense of searing, wounded intimacy. . . . Both actors speak this soaring, voluptuous, difficult text with that finest of techniques which is based on artistic intelligence and true human feeling: two massive but golden performances from a golden age.' It is John Peter, too, who picks up on 'one of Hall's finest achievements . . . [which is] to show us the sinew and muscle of politics and the compelling force of unspoken arguments'.

That Hall had waited to do the play until he had the 'leaders' he wanted for his cast is further validated by Irving Wardle of *The Times* ('for the first time in living memory, the English stage has two actors capable of doing full justice to the roles . . . their detail and speed is electrifying . . .'). Coveney writes: 'The range of this play's scale always seems to escape production. . . . The matching of Judi Dench with Anthony Hopkins proves a triumphant solution to the problem of outlining a failing middle-aged affair, charted with great detail and intimacy, still capable of encompassing the ruin of nations.'

Dench's Cleopatra is variously hailed as capricious, volatile, able to 'somersault her emotions like a whirling acrobat', enchanting, exuberant, imperious, in a performance of 'fearless self-exposure' and carnality. The latter is 'not a familiar weapon in Judi Dench's armoury,' Coveney reminds us, and for Milton Shulman (*Evening Standard*) it is 'a surprising triumph that . . . one of nature's Englishwomen . . . so splendidly achieved the sexual abandon, feline cunning, passionate jealousy, and unquenchable possessiveness of a Mediterranean Queen'. Steve Grant called her 'the ultimate siren, part-bitch, part-sadist, robust, horny'.

For Michael Ratcliffe (*Observer*) she is 'glorious . . . scornful, sassy, blessed with terrific energy, temper and wit. The head swerves with the speed of a snake or a bird at the first hint of a reverse; the round grinning face slumps into a thunderous, sullen and cruelly ageing mask when more seriously put out . . . she has fashioned [the part] to suit her gifts . . . has kept her Antony . . . by sexuality and intelligence combined, and by her irresistible, dark-throated, broken laugh.'

Peter Kemp relishes that she 'also keeps you aware of Cleopatra's tawdrinesses – the peevish insecurity of the mistress behind the swagger of the Queen, the crafty calculation and occasional panic, the stagey luxuriatings in her own performances. Posturing before her court like the amorous star-turn of the Mediterranean Basin. . . .'

Coveney notes 'the savage resentment' with which she reacts to Antony's death, after which her fifth act becomes 'a riveting emotional journey from tragic self-pity to the ecstatic embrace of death in marmoreal splendour'. For Billington: 'Ms Dench even gets over the notorious hurdle of the last Act. . . . *By looking for the precise meaning of each speech* [my italics] . . . [she] goes to her death with single-minded certainty.'

Over Anthony Hopkins' portrayal, viewpoints differ: while Ratcliffe calls Antony 'an affectionate, exhausted and introspective old lion . . . frankly a bit short on the sex and fun', and for some he is 'somnambulant', others see 'a restless prowler', 'extraordinarily light on his feet'.

With the kind of gratuitous malice that debases criticism, Peter Kemp's review is headed 'Lady and the Worm', and goes on to complain: 'Where the play signals Antony's teetering towards collapse by abrupt changes of mood – from rant to realism, tear-jerking sentimentality to sour awareness – he remains stolid.' (Obviously Mr Kemp should have been at rehearsals when the actor was at his drunken best!) Wardle, on the other hand, praises Hopkins for that very resistance to 'all the invitations to rage and despair . . . the magnitude of the performance is that of a man with too much dignity to exhibit his real despair to his followers'. Along similar lines, Shulman finds that it is the promise of 'spectacular eruptions' in 'this smouldering volcano of a man that . . . constantly fascinates us. . . .'

For Grant in *Time Out*, 'his broody mannerisms chillingly convey a soldier caught in the web not merely of *amour* but of time, and in certain scenes (the whipping of the messenger from Octavius), he raises the play to hitherto-unfelt heights'. It is a response echoed by Billington: 'What I shall remember most is Mr Hopkins' false gaiety – and overpowering inward grief – in the short scene where he bids farewell to his servants . . . the knowledge of death sits on Antony; and when Mr Hopkins says he will contend even with his pestilent scythe it is with a swashbuckling bravura that moves one to tears.'

Tim Pigott-Smith's 'excellent Octavius is a frigid but choleric politician . . . devious but self-righteous' (John Peter), 'a pasty virginal marionette, flinching from contact . . . formidable, though, the certain winner in the field' (Ratcliffe), 'livid, leering', 'awkwardly regal' and 'a glowering youth'. Wardle sees 'a brilliant study in graceless tension', Billington appreciates that his Octavius is not 'the usual cold prig but . . . a man who combines calculation with passion: it is a superb study of a power-lover who delights in spotting and playing on other men's flaws'. As 'a marvellous performance [it] sets the standard for the rest of a very strong and well-knit cast' (Coveney).

For John Peter, Michael Bryant's Enobarbus, 'a brilliant portrayal of powerful feelings held in check by a sober, soldierly manner, shows more closely than any other performance I've seen that this blunt, cautious man is the moral touchstone of both the politics and the emotions of the play'. He is 'tender, smiling and subtly proletarian . . . half in love with Cleopatra throughout' (Ratcliffe), more obviously 'grizzled, world-weary' and 'a jaunty Cockneyfied soldier – like something out of Kipling – with a veteran line in gruff cynicism' (Kemp). His description of her first meeting with Antony has a 'marvelling, quiet recall', is 'freshly conceived' and (Ratcliffe again) 'rarely . . . so simply and full-heartedly done'.

Amongst 'a strong cast who speak Shakespeare's verse better than we are used to hearing it spoken today, Basil Henson, Mike Hayward and Brian Spink stand out' (Osborne). I have already mentioned the praise Henson's unusual interpretation elicited – a general on whom '[Caesar's] dishonesties are not lost'. David Schofield is 'a lethally impetuous Pompey', Jerry Flynn 'an affecting Eros', Miranda Foster and Helen Fitzgerald are said to play the handmaidens excellently and Sally Dexter is 'a suppressed Octavia, white-faced with fury'. John Bluthal's doubling as 'a jovial Lepidus and the rustic fellow with the worms' is mentioned both in the press and on radio. The strength of the production, Billington feels, is the way in which every role has been reconsidered.

There are numerous references to Alison Chitty's sets and costumes – 'russet for the autumnal pomp of Egypt, steel blue for Rome' – which 'handsomely indicate the differing emotional temperatures of the two antagonistic cultures'. Along with the 'glittering highlights and bold, leaping shadows' of Stephen Wentworth's lighting, they are praised for the way in which they add to the clarity and frame the momentous events of the play. 'This is a grown-ups' art of Venetian sensuality, experience and amplitude' (Ratcliffe). Although Coveney feels that Wentworth's lighting is 'over-endowed with impertinent shadows', Osborne finds it natural and poetic.

I am only surprised that, apart from a reference to 'thrilling drum rolls', there has not been a general recognition of the extent to which Muldowney's music has contributed to the dramatic, emotional – and aural – resonance of the play.

Other than that, as a composite body, the critics recognize virtually every aspect of the production's intentions. In the words of Antony, addressing his servants:

> I wish I could be made so many men
> And all of you clapped up together in
> An Antony, that I might do you service. . . .

Hall was later to say how surprised and delighted he was that 'what we were trying to do has been understood – and understood in some complexity'.

By the following Monday morning, once most of the important newspaper reviews are out, no one can pretend to be less than thrilled by the critical response. Even the actors with smaller parts, who have not had a mention, bask in the knowledge that they are part of a hit.

What I find most striking is that Judi Dench's first comment is 'How wonderful for Peter!' and that this is a sentiment echoed by others I speak to. Nor, I feel, is this mere theatre courtesy; it arises from authentic respect and affection. In the lavish and detailed praise being heaped on the production, it is ultimately Peter Hall's achievement as director which is being recognized – and they are delighted on his behalf.

Many directors get results by stirring up conflict and tension. From the start Hall had created an atmosphere of nurturing calm. He trusted his cast, invited and often incorporated their ideas, whilst offering them his own knowledge and experience. Not only the younger actors but those such as Tony Hopkins, Tim Pigott-Smith and David Schofield feel that he has set a standard for Shakespearean production and performance on which (as Schofield puts it) 'I won't let myself be short-changed in the future!'

Nicki Frei is amassing the reviews as they come in: she, too, refers to the director: he has gone off to the States for a week, having said that the notices did not matter. 'But,' says the publicist, 'when I telephoned to read them to him, he heaved a sigh of relief.'

She also tells a nice anecdote: Tony Hopkins had phoned the National on Saturday to find out which of the Sunday critics had been at the Press Night. Because she was busy, he was put through to one of the other publicists, with whom he had not previously worked: 'Hello,' he said, 'this is Anthony Hopkins. I'm an actor with the National Theatre. . . .'

CHAPTER 13

In Repertoire – and After

Selected quotes from the press – including the irresistible 'Judi Dench and Anthony Hopkins giving the performance of their lives – and of ours, too' (*Sunday Times*) – were incorporated into the next printing of the theatre's booking brochure.

But an audience hardly needed to be wooed: *Antony and Cleopatra* had become a 'hot ticket'. No sooner had it opened in each six-week period, than priority booking sold out, and queues for day and standing tickets formed from 7.00 in the morning. Scheduled into the NT repertoire until 6 February 1988, the show's one hundred performances would play to capacity, eventually to be seen by 110,000 people.

It would continue to gather accolades: in July, anticipating the summer migration of Americans to Britain, Frank Rich of the *New York Times* would write about a production 'likely to be . . . a landmark': 'Bryant's Enobarbus alone would commend [it] . . . nearly matched by Tim Pigott-Smith's exceptionally human Octavius Caesar'. In August, *Time* magazine called it 'simply the best show in town . . . a magnificent staging'. Hopkins and Dench 'make the roles their own for a generation – and remind all who watch them of why Broadway views London with esteem and envy'. Again tribute is paid to Pigott-Smith ('a very archetype of the smiling lethal pragmatist'), to Bryant ('who, in the play's most spectacular moment, evokes an entire great battle just by his eyes' fearful reaction to its distant lights and noise'), as well as to John Bluthal's Lepidus ('a magnificent hack with keen survival instincts').

At the Evening Standard Drama Awards in November 1987, Sir Peter Hall, by 'an unarguable consensus', became Best Director for *Antony and Cleopatra*, and Judi Dench, Best Actress. Anthony

Hopkins was one of the main candidates for Best Actor (which went to Michael Gambon in another NT production, *A View from the Bridge*). In January 1988, at the Laurence Olivier Awards, Dench was again named Best Actress for her Cleopatra and Michael Bryant was recognized for his 'Outstanding Performance of the Year in a Supporting Role' both as Enobarbus and as the Earl of Gloucester in *King Lear*. It was in January, too, in the New Year's Honours list, that Dench was made a Dame of the British Empire, joining Dame Peggy Ashcroft (1956) and Dame Wendy Hiller (1975) as actresses thus accredited: that this was in the year of her Cleopatra is, I imagine, more than mere coincidence.

After its Press Night and throughout its run, I went back again – and then again – to see *Antony and Cleopatra*. It became quite addictive, so fascinated was I by the growth to maturity, in both individuals and the company as a whole, once they had, in Peter Hall's words, 'bedded in'. The more familiar the vast span of the play, the better the actors became at pacing themselves along it, building towards the big emotional moments and allowing themselves to enjoy the subtleties in those that were quieter or more cerebral. Crevices in understanding were filled out. As words, sense, and emotion became inseparably intertwined, one's response was a deep satisfaction at the absolute logic, clarity and 'rightness' of the cohesion.

In the first half of the play, Tim Pigott-Smith's Caesar becomes a riveting picture of unease, every awkward gesture, every curbed phrase contributing to the sense of a man struggling to find his space in the shadow of a boyhood hero. Part Two crystallizes into a vendetta against Antony for having disillusioned him and abused his sister and, because it is so intensely personalized, makes credible the emotion aroused by Antony's death. Now there is a genuine feeling of loss – even if it be loss of the conflict between them.

As with all the actors, increasingly specific use is made of a physical environment which has become wholly familiar. In the scene on Pompey's galley Caesar watches Antony's antics with a mixture of envy and disapproval, *clutching the rope rigging overhead*. Still holding on to a rope, he then turns to stare moodily – and queasily – out to sea, both isolated from and braced against human contact.

As an example of rethought detail which makes a difference:

Schofield no longer wears his billowing cloak on Pompey's first entrance (reserving it for the ceremonial meeting with the Triumvirate). Instead, his leather doublet is open, exposing a flashy waistcoat and a scarf knotted round his neck. The effect is piratical, a touch of *The Wild Bunch* – and makes him far more at one with his brigand band.

As if I had never sat through the play before, I am struck, again and again, by the heartstopping beauty of its poetry – such as Cleopatra's lines when Thidias is announced:

> What no more ceremony? See my women,
> Against the blown rose may they stop their nose
> That kneeled unto the buds.

This is dependent not only on Dench, but on the general lucidity in the playing, which has led one to respond to 'the sensual nature of language, arising out of deep emotion, physicalized in words', for which Hall had hoped.

The appeal to sight, touch, smell and sound in Bryant's description of Cleopatra in her barge awakens everything that is joyous and romantically blissful. 'For her own person . . .': he seems at a loss for words, flings a leg over the arm of the chair he is sitting on, rubs a hand across his eyes, as if to dispel a mirage. The stage darkens, until he and his listeners are in a ring of light, encircled by deep shadows. He plants each thought, each image with deliberation: 'Age cannot wither her . . .', and one leans forward for the next . . . The language – put across in a performance which is so accessible, so economical – causes frissons of delight. It is gratitude for gifts bestowed that the audience are expressing through their spontaneous applause at the end of the scene.

More than anything, the relationship between Cleopatra and Antony becomes deep-rooted: it was in the later Thidias scene that something had triggered between Dench and Hopkins which, for me, told its truth. Hopkins was now playing Antony, in defeat, as swashbuckling, wilful, dangerous. Accusing Cleopatra of being 'a boggler ever', what had formerly been only verbal now becomes, by inevitable extension, physical abuse – he pushes, prods and shoves at her, and, for all her spirit, Cleopatra suddenly seems powerless. (I even have a glimpse of a battered wife.) Mimicking how she let Caesar's ambassador kiss her hand, Antony also kisses it – then spits.

When the bloodied Thidias is brought back, Antony lies down beside him, luxuriating in his power to punish. It is horrendous Roman sadism and the 'soft' Alexandrians are repelled. Finally, when Cleopatra kneels on the floor to protest her love for him, Antony strolls out of the room. Just when one thinks he has gone for ever, he returns to stand behind her and at last accepts her words: 'I am satisfied'. At that moment, Cleopatra collapses into helpless sobs. He kneels to comfort her, cradling her in his arms. . . .

A blinding light is cast on their relationship: neurotic, all-consuming and obsessional, it is far beyond the realms of reason or judgement. This is indeed Shakespeare's 'madness of love', the 'vagaries of passion . . . the quite intolerable ways men and women treat each other when they are emotionally and sexually dependent on one another', as spoken of by Hall.

With *Antony and Cleopatra*, Hall and his company were taking on a pretty impossible play: it is like a huge novel, covering enormous tracts of territory and involving extraordinary, larger-than-life characters. What is fine in the reading, where one can make the leaps of imagination needed, is a problem to stage convincingly. The first task was to find a scenic solution, and then to carve out against it the human complexity, the blood-and-guts of the characters. . . .

First something is discussed intellectually (for example, the strain in Cleopatra and Antony's relationship in Part Two of the play). This remains a hovering concept until tested for validity. Then it begins to take root emotionally and be scored into performance.

Many decisions are made with conviction at one stage in rehearsal, only to be reversed later (a good example being Antony's drunkenness in the scene with the servants). There is a sense in which the ghosts of these alternative choices throw the one ultimately fixed upon into stronger relief.

What appears in performance is only the tip of a broad-based iceberg. When you go to the theatre, what you see is the culmination of weeks of rehearsal, during which countless discoveries have been made about the way the story unfolds, about the particular interplay of characters which has forced the action in one direction rather than another. If the process has been truly creative, each actor will have uncovered innumerable possibilities for his or her character, and will have a widely-accrued background from which to draw.

The opening night, then, is only a demarcation point along the way – every rehearsal run-through before it, each performance after, will be a fusion of the choices being made, moment to moment, by each of the characters involved. A production is in a continual state of dynamism and you must know, in seeing it, that it is only one cross-section of a sphere with which you are being presented – or can take in at a single sitting. In order to do justice to it and yourself, you should really return to see alternative cross-sections: only then could you have some measure of the richness beneath. And this is, for me, the truly ephemeral nature of the theatre.

Although theatre is traditionally an ephemeral experience, it is hard to accept that every major production is not filmed or videoed as a matter of course, that, in this day and age, there will not be a lasting record on tape of Peter Hall's *Antony and Cleopatra*. Artistically, it is both tragic and infuriating that important theatre breakthroughs (be they in large or small organizations) do not reach the wider audiences that they could. If there was a video to accompany this book, a single image would cap what I labour to describe.

The mechanics involved are quite simple, but what should be an automatic process founders on contractual complexity. Separate agreements must be negotiated with each creative contributor – actor, director, designer, etc. – as to the charge on their services for 'worldwide buyout', or the percentage of video sales to which each will be entitled. As things stand, most of the costly productions done by the National, the RSC and others disappear without trace other than in the memory of those privileged enough to have caught them live.

That these productions, as well as generating profit for all concerned, could be contributing towards the costs of future productions is part of a wider issue – the need for financial support of the institutions which mount them.

According to its Charter, Britain's (now Royal) National Theatre aims 'to present a diverse repertoire of classic, new and neglected plays from the whole of world drama . . . to do experimental work and work for children and young people, to give audiences a choice of at least six productions at any one time, to take current productions regularly to the regions and abroad, and to use the building to offer a continuous selection of other events in addition to the plays'.

Despite being an institution, and despite establishment support, the NT has fought to be unintimidating and accessible – not least by maintaining a low-priced seat structure. In 1987, a quarter of available tickets cost £7 or less;* there are reductions for matinées and previews, for day seats, for students, school parties, pensioners and the unemployed.

Because of the nature of the plays it does, and the turnover of productions within the repertoire, the National's box office income, even at 90–100 per cent capacity, will never be enough to cover expenditure. Hence government subsidy – via the Arts Council of Great Britain and *sufficient to maintain the standards expected of a 'national' theatre* – is a *sine qua non*. Yet this remains contentious, its case endlessly having to be battled out by those in the field.

The 1986/87 Arts Council grant to the NT was £7.8 million. At the end of 1986 (having had to plan for the forthcoming year in the usual limbo of financial uncertainty) the NT was told that the 1987/88 grant would be exactly the same (in real terms, of course, given annual inflation, a decrease on the preceding year).† Running costs and maintenance of the South Bank building alone consume £1 million a year, and spiralling labour and material costs, wage increases to actors and technicians, rising charges for advertising etc., have worsened the situation. When the theatre is forced to compromise its aims, it is usually the result of a funding crisis: this caused Hall, in 1985, to close the Cottesloe for four months (until an extra grant from the now-defunct Greater London Council bridged the financial gap). Touring, involving heavy additional expenses, has had to be curtailed. . . .

'I am absolutely bewildered,' said Hall. 'We don't have a deficit, we've balanced our books and our thanks for it is that we have a funding cut. What it means for us is that eventually there will be less and less productions. And meanwhile, we're not mending the roof.'

Critic Michael Billington, in the *Guardian* (December 1986), wrote of 'talent being exploited, energy being drained and vision being impaired. How can you plan for the future when your back is

* £8.50 by 1989.
† In 1988/89 the grant was £7.9 million and in 1989/90, £8.6 million – minimal increases.

permanently against the wall?'* His claim that the theatre is 'largely made up of dedicated nutters who put art before profit' is justified: I have always believed that those who put artistic effort and sheer number of work-hours into making theatre available are, in fact, subsidizing the public; the financial compensation is way below what they might earn, for comparable expertise and overtime, elsewhere.

Each year the NT aims to make up the balance of subsidy with self-earned income, roughly pound for pound (in 1986/87, about 44 per cent of the total year's costs). This is mainly from the box office, but also includes television rights to NT productions, profits from NT publications (NT videos, too, some day?), from catering and other front-of-house services. In conjunction with a commercial producer, highly successful productions (such as *Amadeus*, *Guys and Dolls*, *Brighton Beach Memoirs* and *A View from the Bridge*) are transferred to the West End or Broadway for an open-ended run, and the NT receives a percentage of the box-office take.

Nevertheless, the National Theatre's product is not primarily about commercial viability and has to be protected from the pressure to become so. Decrying the checks and frustrations of a government policy that seems to regard theatre as a disposable luxury rather than a spiritual necessity, '"bums-on-seats" is *not* a philosophy', wrote Billington sharply.

In July 1989, in a full-page article in *The Times*, Peter Hall dealt comprehensively with the biting effect which ten years of Thatcherism have had on the performing arts.

During the forty years since the Second World War, subsidy had fertilized a rich creativity, possibly 'a golden age of British drama, quite as fruitful as that of the Elizabethans'. By giving grants below the inflation level, this government is systematically de-stabilizing the subsidized theatre and destroying what had been gained: 'the puritans have triumphed once again, though this time they believe in Mammon rather than God, in market values rather than visions . . . if an enterprise does not make money or – as in the case of subsidized

---

* In November 1988 Arts Minister Richard Luce announced the introduction of three-year funding. Arts Council clients, the National amongst them, had been lobbying for this for years and now have the opportunity to plan forward on a more realistic footing. In 1989 he persuaded the Government to put an additional £12 million into funding of the Arts.

theatre – does not *appear* to make money, it is suspect [and] probably unnecessary'.

Hall feels that, having pushed the arts to go after private sponsorship in 'a mixed economy', and (despite assurances to the contrary) reduced public funding as a result, the present Tory regime is responsible for 'one of the worst betrayals that any government has perpetrated on its artists'. It is inevitable that increasing dependence on hand-outs from the private sector will affect theatre policy, that in order to survive, artistic directors will make choices in line with what the sponsor and his customers approve – in general the non-challenging and 'respectable'. The threat to the National Theatre is that 'its primary aim will not be how to serve the public and its charter, but simply how to balance the books'.

Earlier in the piece, Hall says: 'A democracy not adult enough to spend a fair proportion of its money on its artists without objecting when they are critical, is not a healthy democracy'. He concludes on a passionate note: 'We need art desperately. It is not only spiritual food, it is a way of keeping our democracy robust. The simplifications of modern government seem to demand to be answered by the complexities of art.'

Antony and Cleopatra was produced within an existent organization. There was an on-going superstructure to service it, one of the many productions in the National's repertoire running for a fixed period of time. Thus administrative, technical and operational costs (of marketing and box office, print and publicity, workshop facilities and labour etc.) would all be built into the National Theatre's overheads, as would the salaries of the company doing the play – director, designers, actors and stage management. This is very different from a fringe theatre or repertory company doing plays in sequence, where costs are attributed on a one-by-one basis – or from a commercial management raising financial backing to do a West End show which, if successful, may run for years until all its audience potential has been tapped.

Production Expenditure: *Antony and Cleopatra*

Sets and Props		£43,195
Contract Labour		22,090
Costumes		46,250
(including 120 costumes	£37,000	
30 suits armour	9,000)	

Total cost of physical staging: Actual –   111,500
                                 (Budget –   111,100)
Box Office gross by end of run: £951,000

This was an expensive production, undoubtedly, but I would say that the only indulgence was that of the time spent for rehearsal – a real luxury which every other theatre would envy. I am no lover of large theatre institutions; in fact, my own preference is for new writing in an intimate space (a Robert Holman play at the Bush, for instance). But there is something incomparable about seeing one of the great classical plays in the appropriately epic setting of a large arena stage.

Almost ten years ago, Michael Coveney used a phrase which I have never forgotten: 'studio conditions are prohibitive to the digging of roots in the collective imagination'. We need to be reminded of the Promethean and heroic. There is a hunger for the almost religious experience of seeing human drama, human tragedy, writ bold and thrilling. This is the hunger which was once satisfied by the classical drama on which our traditions are based and it is only large institutions possessed of grand spaces, and with the financial resources able to rise to the necessary degree of largesse – in set, costumes and, indeed, numbers of actors – that can aspire to these great theatrical experiences.*

In his article for *The Times*, Hall said: 'It is interesting that with the new philistinism there exists another contradictory trend. We pore over the art of the past, striving to find its original meaning, its original form. It is as if, lacking any firm beliefs or faiths of our own, we are ransacking the past for reassurance. To this end, art has become almost a religion.'

An important function of the National is to provide for these needs, in just such productions as *Antony and Cleopatra* – not bijou, not innovative, not idiosyncratic, but played 'straight', as true as possible to Shakespeare's own vision. Perhaps this is what Hall meant when he said, on one occasion, 'This is not a period production. It is very much of the eighties and could not have been done at any other time.'

---

* For the widest audiences, of course, films have usurped the territory: think of D. W. Griffith, Cecil B. de Mille, Eisenstein, *Gone with the Wind*, *Lawrence of Arabia*, *2001 – Space Odyssey*, *Apocalypse Now*, *Ghandi*. . .

It was also important that his Cleopatra and his Antony brought with them their own eminence: Dench who has achieved a royal status in the theatre, whose many and various performances are stamped upon people's memories years after they saw them, and Hopkins, with his particular charisma, whose transatlantic stardom draws capacity audiences – including to the 1,300-seat Shaftesbury in 1989, when he played there in *M. Butterfly*. The presence of names such as theirs both guarantees the box office take and generates that excitement and mystique which is the essence of 'show business'.

Actors like them are rarely 'resting' (the theatre euphemism for unemployment): after *Antony and Cleopatra* opened, Judi Dench went into rehearsal for Peter Hall's production of *Entertaining Strangers* by David Edgar. She subsequently made her directing debut with *Much Ado* and *Look Back in Anger* for Kenneth Branagh's Renaissance Theatre, played the lead (deliciously!) in a television drama series, *Behaving Badly*, returned to the National to do Gertrude to Daniel Day-Lewis' Hamlet and, by the end of 1989, was starring as Madame Ranyevskaya in *The Cherry Orchard* at the Aldwych.

Anthony Hopkins' career is equally prolific: after alternating the roles of Antony and Lear, he went on to star in the film version of Alan Ayckbourn's *A Chorus of Disapproval*, and a remake of *Great Expectations*. Roles for television included a Welsh farmer in *Heartland* and an intensely moving portrayal of Sir Donald Campbell in *Across the Water*, before he went back into the theatre for *M. Butterfly*, going straight on from there to do two films in America.

As for the rest of the company: not long into the run of *Antony and Cleopatra* the National released Andrew Wadsworth to do *South Pacific* in the West End; once it had ended, David Schofield went off to do the lead in *Me and My Girl*, also a musical, also in the West End. But most of the company stayed on.

Many, including Tim Pigott-Smith and Sally Dexter, were involved in *Entertaining Strangers* and then were able to build on the skills and understanding they had acquired in *Antony and Cleopatra*, when Peter Hall directed them in *Cymbeline*, *The Winter's Tale* and *The Tempest* – for which Alison Chitty was again Hall's designer. Pigott-Smith played a riveting Iachimo, a psychotically jealous Leontes, a dim and disarming Trinculo. Not long afterwards he was invited to become co-director of the late Sir Anthony Quayle's Compass Theatre. Bryant, it seems, is to be a permanent, and ever luminous fixture at the National. His Prospero had been memorable, 'tetchy, querulous, autocratic'. John Peter described his Polonius, in the *Hamlet* which followed, as 'marvellous . . . Observe how the verse keeps its insinuating rhythm but [is] powered by a bounding colloquial drive and shot through with whiplash wit.'

That trio of late Shakespeare plays was to conclude Peter Hall's fifteen-year term at the National, during which he had been responsible for its reputation and stability, at the same time as directing well over twenty works ranging from the ancient Greeks to modern Britons. So it was with an earned satisfaction but considerable relief, that he handed over to Richard Eyre on 1 September 1988.

After *Antony and Cleopatra*, in addition to *Entertaining Strangers* and the three late Shakespeares, he directed *Salome* and *Albert Herring* for Covent Garden, and *Cosi fan Tutte* (the first of three Mozart operas with Simon Rattle conducting) for Glyndebourne, whose artistic director he remains until 1991. His production of Michael Tippett's *New Year* premiered in Houston in late 1989.

Even more significantly, after twenty-five years in the subsidized theatre, Hall left the National to launch the Peter Hall Production Company, a new commercial venture created for him by the English and American impresarios Duncan Weldon and Jerome Minskoff. With the intention of staging classic and contemporary plays on both sides of the Atlantic, he started off with Tennessee Williams' *Orpheus Descending*. Starring Vanessa Redgrave, it packed London's Haymarket Theatre and re-opened in New York. This was followed by *The Merchant of Venice*, with Dustin Hoffman as Shylock and Geraldine James as Portia, which has also been successful, both commercially and critically, in London and New York.

In mid-1989, Hall also completed his eighth film: *She's Been Away*, scripted by Stephen Poliakoff and starring Peggy Ashcroft, Geraldine James and James Fox. At time of writing, plans for the future tumble over one another: two American classics, two new British plays, a piece by Edna O'Brien on the Irish nationalist, Maud Gonne, a dramatisation of Richmal Crompton's William stories, a musical version of Ionesco's *Rhinoceros*, a co-production with the Greek National Theatre, of *The Trojan Women*, to be staged at Epidaurus at dawn, an all-night production of *Mourning Becomes*

Electra in New York, more Ibsen, more Chekhov, some Shaw, plenty of Shakespeare. . . .

The man is unstoppable, an obsessive workaholic. As the last of Britain's great postwar director/managers, through the companies he created and the plays he has directed, he has given us great gifts; obviously we can anticipate many more.

Plutarch and Harley Granville Barker

As background reading for his cast, Peter Hall recommended North's translation of Plutarch and Harley Granville Barker's Preface to *Antony and Cleopatra*.

The source for the play was Plutarch's *Life of Marcus Antonius*. Written c. AD 80, in the century after the events occurred (Antony and Cleopatra met in 41 BC, died in 30 BC), it is a combination of eye-witness reports, via Plutarch's grandfather, who knew a physician studying in Alexandria when Antony was there, and the records of, amongst others, Cleopatra's personal physician Olympus. Plutarch had himself visited Egypt, so that much of his writing has the vividness of personal reminiscence.

Sir Thomas North's translation (1579) provides a fascinating insight into Shakespeare's dramatic construction and creation of character. One sees how he absorbed all the information provided by Plutarch and adapted it to his own purposes, switching the order and combination of events, deciding which to dramatize, which to present through oblique report and which to omit entirely. (Shakespeare also steals great chunks from Plutarch and puts them into blank verse.) He selects his characters from a host of possibilities, chooses when to introduce them to strongest effect, and fleshes out those to whom Plutarch accorded a passing mention (of whom Enobarbus is a supreme example). Rather like reading the original novel from which a magnificent film has been carved, it makes rewarding reading.

Harley Granville Barker (1877–1946), actor, director and playwright, had a deep understanding of the articulation of a Shakespearean play, combining practical staging advice with scholarship. From his Preface to *Antony and Cleopatra* one gets rich and frequently poetic insights into the play's construction, language and character development. The Preface also gave Hall and Alison Chitty a concept for set and costume designs which meshed with their own thinking. From Granville Barker's writing:

> For Shakespeare's audiences the actors were very plainly on the stage, but the characters might, half the time, be nowhere in particular. It was, for the dramatist of the day, a privilege akin to the novelist's, who may, if he chooses, detach characters, through page after page, from fixed surroundings. It was a freedom which the promise of the scenic stage gradually sapped . . . [when] change of scene did not mean change of scenery, there was no distracting of mind or eye . . . and the action flowed on unchecked.
>
> . . . in this play, quite evidently, Roman and Egyptian stood in picturesque contrast . . . Rome meant the romantic past, Egypt the exotic East; and Shakespeare would do what he could to capitalize both . . . Our concern is with the Egypt and Rome of his imagination, not of our own.
>
> In the National Gallery hangs Paolo Veronese's *Alexander and the Wife and Daughter of Darius*. This will be very much how Shakespeare saw his Roman figures habited. . . .
>
> Cleopatra's are the coquetries of a great lady of [Shakespeare's] own time . . . What then is the solution of this problem, if the sight of the serpent of old Nile in a farthingale will too dreadfully offend us? We can compromise. Look at Tintoretto's and Paolo Veronese's paintings of 'classic' subjects. We accept them readily enough. . . .

INDEX

A figure 2 after a page number means that there are two separate references to the subject on that page.